AUTOBIOGRAPHY

OF

SILAS THOMPSON TROWBRIDGE M. D.

T0046464

Shawnee Classics
A Series of Classic Regional Reprints for the Midwest

AUTOBIOGRAPHY

OF

SILAS THOMPSON TROWBRIDGE M. D.

With a New Introduction by
John S. Haller Jr. and Barbara Mason

SOUTHERN ILLINOIS UNIVERSITY PRESS
Carbondale

Printed in the United States of America
07 06 05 04   4 3 2 1

Library of Congress Cataloging-in-Publication Data
 Trowbridge, Silas Thompson, 1826–1893.
  Autobiography of Silas Thompson Trowbridge, M.D. / with
a new introduction by John S. Haller and Barbara Mason.
     p. cm. — (Shawnee classics)
  Originally published: Vera Cruz [Mexico] : Family of
Silas Thompson Trowbridge, 1872 [sic, 1874].
   1. Surgeons—United States—Biography. I. Haller, John S.
II. Mason, Barbara, 1926– III. Title. IV. Series.
   RD27.35.T75T76 2004
   617'.092—dc22
   [B]
   ISBN 0-8093-2591-8 (alk. paper)   2004056497

Printed on recycled paper. ♻

The paper used in this publication meets the minimum
requirements of American National Standard for Information Sciences—Permanence of Paper for Printed Library
Materials, ANSI Z39.48-1992. ∞

Reprinted from the original 1874 edition.

INTRODUCTION

This book, of which only a handful of the original edition remains in circulation, came to the attention of Southern Illinois University Press by way of the Ulysses S. Grant Association. The book was printed on a small hand press that the author, Silas Thompson Trowbridge, M.D., had purchased for his children. The outcome of the family's efforts was the *Autobiography of Silas Thompson Trowbridge M.D.* which, aside from frequent grammatical mistakes and an erroneous publishing date of 1872 (instead of 1874), provides a fascinating window into America's past. Trowbridge's reminiscences of his early life, his marriage and medical practice, his experiences as a regimental surgeon in the Civil War, and later, as United States Consul, make interesting reading for both the casual as well as the serious reader.

Silas Trowbridge was born in Indiana in 1826 of parents who had emigrated from New York. His father had served his country as an infantry captain along the Canadian frontier in 1814, and his mother's ancestors had settled originally in pre-revolutionary Vermont. When Silas's mother died, his father converted the family's holdings into land that he then distributed to the three sons.

At sixteen, Silas began teaching school in Indiana, a career that he interspersed with farming, selling horses, and driving cattle. In 1845, he moved to Heyworth, Illinois, where he continued to teach but, in addition, commenced the study of medicine as a pleasant pastime. On returning to eastern Indiana the next year, he exchanged his eighty acres of land in Blackford County for stock in the White Water Valley Canal Company, which unfortunately failed. Stung by his financial setback, Silas once again took up the study of medicine, this time in earnest, using his earnings from a two-month tour of driving cattle to pay for instruments and an apprenticeship in the home of Dr. Harrison Noble in Le Roy, Illinois.

At the age of twenty-three, after fourteen months of reading medical texts and assisting in the practice of Dr. Noble, Silas went out on his own, opening a practice near New Castle, Illinois. Disappointed in his prospects, he moved to Decatur, a town of approximately seven hundred inhabitants and the county seat of Macon County, where he proceeded to build a respected practice. As with other so-called regular physicians of his day, Trowbridge treated patients with the traditional remedies of bleeding, antiphlogistics, emetics, and cathartics.

Although accepted by the community, young Dr. Trowbridge lacked a medical degree and, recognizing its importance in an age of increasing competitiveness, especially from sectarian or irregular doctors, he left Decatur in 1850 to attend a four-month course of medical lectures at Rush Medical College in Chicago. The college, named in honor of Dr. Benjamin Rush, physician and statesman of Philadelphia and signer of the Declaration of Independence, was chartered in 1837, organized in 1842, and graduated its first class in 1843.

The founder of the college was Dr. Daniel Brainard (1812–66) of New York. Besides Brainard, the faculty included Dr. Nathan Smith Davis (1817–1904), formerly of New York City, who accepted the chair of physiology and pathology and who lectured daily throughout the term and also met students each day in the hospital wards. Davis was largely responsible for founding the American Medical Association and its journal, the Chicago Medical College (Northwestern University Medical Department), and the *Chicago Medical Journal*. Other Rush faculty when Trowbridge arrived included doctors Joseph W. Freer, John Evans, Graham N. Fitch, Austin Flint, Ephraim Ingals, William B. Herrick, and Thomas Spencer.

By 1850, Rush Medical College had given instruction to 532 students and awarded the doctor of medicine to 132 of them. The 1850 session had 104 students in attendance, of whom 42 graduated. The cost of Dr. Trowbridge's schooling included $35 in course fees, a dissection ticket (optional but strongly recommended) for $5, and tickets for clinical work in the United States Marine Hospital and the Illinois General Hospital of the Lakes that were free.

At the time of Trowbridge's attendance, Chicago had a population of approximately twenty-eight thousand inhabitants. Rush was the only medical college in Illinois until 1859, when Lind University (now Northwestern University Medical School) was established. Other schools that had formed in Illinois either closed or moved away. These included Illinois College Medical School of Jacksonville, which existed from 1843 to 1848; Franklin Medical College in St. Charles, which operated from 1842 to 1849; and the Rock Island Medical School, which organized in 1848 and moved the following year to Davenport, Iowa.

Three years' study and two annual terms of sixteen weeks each were required for graduation. A course of lectures consisted of four morning lectures of an hour each, followed by four afternoon lectures of the same length. Of the various areas taught by the college, surgery became increasingly well known. When students were not spending their spare time studying human anatomy in the college's dissecting rooms, they were enjoying the sights and sounds of this bustling city on Lake Michigan. Because of Trowbridge's previous experience, he was permitted to graduate after attending a single course of lectures and writing a twenty-page thesis. Interestingly, he also was the ghostwriter for another student's thesis, no doubt a commentary on the lack of quality control in medical colleges of the day and the fact that his fellow student lacked the requisite skills to write a thesis.

While attending lectures, Trowbridge and several of his classmates boarded at the home of a young widow, Mrs. Emeline Henderson, whom Trowbridge soon married. At the time, circulars advertised room and board for medical students in local homes for $1.50 to $2.00 per week. On returning to Decatur with his new wife, Dr. Trowbridge formed a partnership with Dr. W. J. Chenoweth and, later, Dr. George Beman. He also brought a young family relative into his home as his first student apprentice.

In the mid-1850s, Trowbridge took the lead in bringing together the regular medical men of Macon County, Illinois, to form a county medical society in conformity with the rules established by the newly formed American Medical Association and the Illinois State Medical Society. He served as secretary and treasurer for the county society and contributed several papers at its meetings.

In 1859 and 1860, Trowbridge sought the passage of a law prohibiting incompetent persons from practicing medicine and another one that would legalize dissections. With respect to the latter, the State Medical Society established a committee that included both Trowbridge and his former teacher, Nathan S. Davis, to work directly with the Illinois General Assembly. Both legislative efforts, however, failed to garner sufficient support and the ensuing political crisis and Civil War years buried both issues for years.

Also, on January 3, 1860, Trowbridge patented a "Cane for Physicians" (Pat. No. 26,721) that consisted of a hollow wooden tube sealed at the bottom and designed as a receptacle for ten vials containing medicines. The invention was intended for country physicians who were compelled to carry their medicines in cumbersome saddlebags or chests. The knob or handle of the cane consisted of an ink bottle, thus providing the physician with access to additional ink in the event he had to leave the patient with a prescription or written directions. To Trowbridge's dismay, the medical cane was never manufactured.

The election of Lincoln on November 6, 1860 and the secession of the southern states brought major changes in Trowbridge's life. When shore batteries opened fire on Fort Sumter on April 12, 1861, he dissolved his eighteen-month partnership with Dr. Beman and, on April 25, signed up for three months' service as a surgeon of the 8th Illinois Volunteer Infantry commanded by Colonel Richard J. Oglesby (1824–99). As Trowbridge explained, the numbers of the Illinois regiments in the Civil War commenced where the numbers of the regiments that were engaged in the Mexican War left off. Thus, the first regiment of the war was numbered "seven," the second, "eight," and so on.

The 8th Illinois Volunteers was immediately ordered to Cairo, Illinois, where they were involved in several small expeditions to Cape Girardeau, Commerce, Bloomfield, and Norfolk, Missouri, and to Paducah and Blandville, Kentucky, before being mustered out. On July 25, 1861, the regiment was reorganized and mustered in for three years' service.

When Grant faced off against the Confederates at the Battle of Belmont (November 7, 1861) in Missouri, Trowbridge made his "debut at the operating table" in Cairo where he received many of the battle's casualties. Trowbridge observed that he saw more deaths from disease at Cairo than at any other time during the war. Following the Battle of Belmont, General Grant moved against Fort Henry, a Confederate earthen fort on the Tennessee River (February 6, 1862). Its fall opened the Tennessee River all the way to Muscle Shoals, Alabama, to Union gunboats and shipping. In this battle, Colonel Oglesby was given the first brigade and Trowbridge served as his aide.

Fort Donelson on the Cumberland was regarded by Confederate General Albert S. Johnson as the major defense of Nashville. After a four-day siege (February 12–16) by the Union forces, the fort surrendered unconditionally to Grant. The victory ensured that Kentucky would stay in the Union and opened Tennessee to Grant's advance. Trowbridge first saw action under fire during this siege and was responsible for arranging temporary hospitals for the wounded in the rear of each regiment of the brigade. The condition of the men on both sides was made worse by the weather—cold, sleet, and snow. The losses of the 8th Illinois Infantry included 56 killed in battle, 187 wounded, 13 prisoners, and 80 cases of frost-bite from exposure.

Among the wounded was Colonel John A. Logan (1826–86), formerly from the Illinois State House (1852) and U.S. Representative (1859–62), commanding the 31st Illinois Volunteers. Shot in the left shoulder, he was treated with Dover's Powders (powder of ipecac and opium), an anodyne used to induce sweating and reduce fever, and doses of calomel and opium, all of which had a deleterious effect on him. Taking control of the case, Trowbridge prescribed turpentine taken internally, with clysters (enemas), and frictions of the same medicine. His choice of turpentine (terebinthina) was not particularly unusual. The oil or spirits of turpentine was a popular cure-all in nineteenth-century therapeutics, particularly when other medicines were scarce. With it, doctors claimed to have successfully treated almost all the known diseases of humankind and beast. Given orally, rectally, through the skin, by inhalation, and even by injection, turpentine remained popular among American doctors well into the 1880s. So great was its popularity that it competed with the trio of calomel, opium, and tartar emetic, known as the "north stars of therapia." In tablespoon doses it acted as a purgative; in teaspoon doses it served as a diuretic; in doses of fifteen to twenty drops as a nervine and anodyne; in ten drops as an aseptic; and in single doses of five drops to facilitate digestion. Doctors treated sprains, bruises, and swollen joints with a turpentine liniment and poured the oil over open wounds to prevent gangrene and tetanus. During the Civil War, physicians frequently substituted turpentine for the more expensive quinine.[1]

Trowbridge had a poor opinion of Logan because he was an "open enemy" of Oglesby and because he gave Trowbridge only "coy acknowledgement" for his help when wounded. Loyal to his regimental commander and proud of his own medical abilities, Trowbridge described Logan as a "selfish cold blooded man, who doubtlessly feels that he has shed condescending honor upon his medical attendant in allowing him the privilege of treating such a distinguished personage." Logan survived his battle injuries and returned to Washington as the United States representative (1867–71) and senator (1871–77; 1879–86) and as a candidate for the vice presidency during the 1884 campaign.

Trowbridge used his *Autobiography* to correct some of the early histories written of the war's great battles. Reflecting on the Battle of Fort Donelson, for example, he questioned the veracity of Brigadier General Lewis (Lew) Wallace's (1827–1905) recounting of his role in the victory. From Trowbridge's perspective, Wallace's claims were, "like his fighting, very uncertain." Trowbridge likewise corrected early reports of the

Battle of the Pittsburgh Landing (Shiloh) on April 6–7, 1862, during which the Army of the Tennessee was surprised by the Confederate forces of Albert Sidney Johnson and where some of the harshest fighting took place. Trowbridge pointed out the "disgraceful disregard" by Wallace, then commanding the Federal 3rd Division some six miles from Pittsburgh Landing, of orders sent by General Grant to march to the battlefield. Although Wallace redeemed himself on the second day of the battle, he was harshly criticized for the near disaster of the first day and was sent back to Indiana to await other assignments. Wallace later served as president of the court that tried Captain Henry Wirz, the commandant of the prison at Andersonville, which was the only war crimes trial of the Civil War. Wallace was a member of the military commission that tried the conspirators in Lincoln's assassination; he also served as governor of New Mexico and wrote the popular novel *Ben Hur—A Tale of the Christ* (1880).

In his reminiscences, Trowbridge mentions the role of the regiment's drum corpsmen who, during and after the battle, carried wounded to field hospitals where they received temporary medical assistance. The *Regulations for the Army of the United States,* first issued in 1808, established a bifurcated responsibility between the Medical Department and the Quartermaster's Department, leaving management of all transportation of the wounded and the establishment of ambulance depots and hospitals in the hands of the quartermaster. This meant, at best, that a typical regiment of six or seven hundred men would carry into battle a half-dozen ambulance wagons, several hospital tents, and a number of litters. As in earlier wars, convalescents and regimental musicians, including drummers, served as stretcher-bearers. Sometimes this occurred during the battle, but more often in the hours and days following the engagement. Significant is the fact that medical service centered on the needs of the regiment with no plan or system to evacuate the wounded beyond this unit. Upon arrival at the regimental field hospital, the wounded rested on straw or hay strewn around the ground for their comfort while they waited for their turn at the amputating table or for splints, dressings, medicines, and food. The wounded remained at these temporary stations for a week or more before returning to their units, being furloughed home for recuperation, or being evacuated to more permanent hospitals in wagons manned by contract drivers.[2]

Recalling the fighting around Corinth (October 3–4, 1862), when General William S. Rosecrans defeated the combined forces of Generals Sterling Price and Earl Van Dorn, Trowbridge remarked that it took two weeks to clear the wounded from the field, during which time the surgeons were constantly operating. "Our clothes were a gore of blood," he wrote, "and our hands so continuously in it that for most of the time they were crisped and wrinkled like a washerwoman's after a day's labor in her suds." No doubt his Rush medical school course on surgery helped to enlighten him on the basics. But nothing could prepare him for what he faced in the field hospitals of the Civil War. As Trowbridge explained,

> The ligature of the large arteries; amputations from the shoulder joint to the fingers and from the hip joint to the toes; resections, in which a long bone is twice divided and the injured part between the extremities removed and the extremities brought in apposition; exsections, in which an end of a bone leading into a joint is removed and a new end made to take the place of the part removed; extraction of balls, fragments, shells, clothing, splinters of wood, and various articles of foreign substances one may have about his person or of which he may be in the close vicinity, from various parts of the person—even the large cavities such as the brain, lungs, abdomen, etc.; the adjustment and stitching of wounded intestines; the conduct for wounds of the brain, lungs, liver, bladder and spleen; trephining of the skull bones; reductions of fractures and dislocations; extraction or amputation of wounded eyes; secondary operations of all the foregoing, in consequence of Gangrene, Erysipelas, or protrusion of bones; treatment of anemia or prostration from loss or impoverishment of blood; treatment of extensive flesh wounds, bums, scalds and frost-bites; of

severe cases of shock; of Tetanus or Lock-
jaw; of exhausting suppurations; Gangrene, Erysipelas, the various forms of
Fevers and in fine, all the concomitants of
injuries of whatever nature an extensive
and hard fought battle gives.

Gruesome in its details, this sanguinary
litany of surgical duties excluded the dreadful
groans and desolation of the wounded lying without cover or comfort for hours and even days at the
spots where they fell and, as Trowbridge remarked, "where saber and shell and ball and bayonet were the toys of mad men's determinations to
destroy each other." The estimated casualties at
Corinth were 2,359 Union and 4,838 Confederate.

Among the officers wounded at Corinth was
General Oglesby who was in command of his brigade at the time. When Grant heard the news, he
ordered Trowbridge to attend the fallen general
who had been moved to a private house in Corinth.
What ensued was a battle of medical opinions
between Trowbridge and Medical Director J. G. F.
Holsten over the prognosis and the treatment of
the general. It is clear from their differences that
Holsten, formerly a professor of medicine at
Georgetown University, wanted only to comfort
the general until he expired and, as a result, had
little respect for Trowbridge, whom he called "an
upstart" for wanting to do more. Trowbridge's
opinion of Holsten was equally definitive. "How
outrageous and unprofessional" for this man "to
. . . transcend all rules of etiquette and ethics, and

attempt to ride his high official position, and lord it so arrogantly over me," he wrote. Oglesby recovered from his wound and, returning to Illinois after the war, was twice elected governor (1865–69; 1872–73) before becoming United States senator (1873–79) and then elected governor for a third time (1885–89). Oglesby felt indebted to Trowbridge for the attention paid by the young doctor to his injuries and employed him as family physician to his wife and children in the years immediately following the war.

Among the many individuals whom Trowbridge met during the war was Surgeon-General William A. Hammond (1828–1900), credited with recommending the creation of a permanent hospital and ambulance corps, the establishment of an army medical school and permanent general hospital in Washington, and the independence of the Medical Department from the Quartermaster's Department. Pressured by influential members of the United States Sanitary Commission, Secretary of War Edwin M. Stanton reluctantly appointed Hammond to the position of surgeon-general.

A difficult subordinate by any definition of the term, Hammond soon lost the support of his superior when he accused Stanton of showing willful disregard for the comfort of the wounded after the second Battle of Bull Run. Hammond also lost the support of the military and civilian medical profession when, convinced that the excessive use of calomel and tartar emetic had killed more patients than it had helped, he ordered their removal from the official formulary of the U.S. Army. Excessive doses of calomel had caused salivation and tooth loss, while the vomiting and purging caused by tartar emetic (antimony) further debilitated soldiers already weakened by their sickness or wounds. Because medical sectarians such as botanics, eclectics, and homeopaths had long opposed the use of these two medicines, Hammond's decision was attributed to his showing favoritism to irregular medicine.

Trowbridge's own run-in with Hammond followed an invitation from Inspector General Dr. T. F. Perley to become one of his medical inspectors. Because the appointment was to be made from surgeons of the Regular Army or from the Volunteers, it was necessary for Trowbridge, a regimental surgeon, to receive an appointment as surgeon in the Volunteers. This required that he first pass a board of medical examiners and, at Perley's request, he traveled to Washington to meet with the medical board. Before he could be examined, however, Hammond issued an order prohibiting any further examinations for surgeons of Volunteers. Angered by the perceived injustice, Trowbridge returned to his regiment feeling that the surgeon-general had maliciously humbled and disgraced him.

Hammond was burdened with a personality that included both an impulsive temper and a lack of tact. The unsavory mixture eventually resulted in his being court-martialed and found guilty in a particularly vindictive trial. He was subsequently discharged in disgrace from the service. Interestingly, Major General Richard J. Oglesby was president of the military court that found Hammond guilty. In 1863, Oglesby had decided to resign his commission to run for governor of Illinois, and his chairing of the court-martial board was his final duty in the military. It has been suggested by Frank R. Freemon in his *Gangrene and Glory: Medical Care During the American Civil War* (1998) that "this duty was a quid pro quo for [Grant] allowing his resignation and, perhaps, for supporting his candidacy for the Republican nomination for governor."[3]

When news of Hammond's court-martial reached Trowbridge, he remarked that the surgeon-general had "secured the well merited disgrace which a military court-marshal meted out to him, by cashiering him for high crimes and misdemeanors." Not until 1879 did Congress and President Rutherford B. Hayes annul the court's sentence. One may speculate on whether Oglesby's close association with Trowbridge had any effect on the outcome of the court-martial.

Trowbridge was similarly displeased with the quality of medical care given by surgeons in the Confederate army. When several of them were captured during the Battle of Magnolia Church, he ordered medicines and instruments made available to them for attending their wounded. However, as he observed their work, he became visibly troubled by their medical opinions and inferior treatment, concluding that "the great majority of those with whom the collision of arms brought me in contact were of a very inferior grade."

If, by his condescending remark, Trowbridge implied that the Medical Department of the Union army was superior in organization, medical supplies, and evacuation of the wounded, he was correct. But whether the skills of northern physicians were actually better and resulted in improved treatment of the Union's sick and wounded remains unproven. To be sure, the health of the Union army improved and the proportion of sick soldiers diminished as the war went on, while the numbers of Confederates who were disabled by sickness increased. But these differences were the result of better food and improved hygiene, not because of differences in medical education or pedigree. Like Trowbridge, the typical army surgeon of both North and South had attended a single set of four-month lectures and experienced some level of apprenticeship before going into practice. Except among eclectics, botanics, and homeopaths, American medical students were wedded to very traditional techniques and medications, few of which had a decidedly efficacious impact on the patient.

Trowbridge recounted the siege and surrender of Vicksburg, the "Gibraltar of the Mississippi" (May 22–July 4, 1863), where he was appointed surgeon-in-chief. Along with this assignment, Trowbridge was directed to write the surgical proceedings of the Third Division of the Seventeenth Army Corps from the day it left Milikin's Bend to the surrender of Vicksburg. To accomplish his task, Trowbridge had to meet the demands of Dr. John Brinton (1832–1907), the first curator of the Army Medical Museum who was in charge of the medical archives in Washington. Brinton, a brigade surgeon in the Army of the Tennessee, had earlier been responsible for the hospital in Cairo, Illinois. He had evacuated wounded from the Battle of Belmont (Missouri) and had established a hospital on the battlefield of Shiloh. Now stationed in Washington, he was among the staff of army doctors, including Joseph J. Woodward and Joseph K. Barnes, who were charged with preparing a permanent record of the medical experiences of the Civil War.[4]

Trowbridge disliked his new responsibility and accused Brinton of contributing to the "mass of confused rubbish out of which no valuable data could be gathered." He felt the same concerning the later publication of the *Surgical History of the Rebellion (1861–1865),* believing that it could have been a far better documentary of the war had it been more properly handled. Unfortunately, Trowbridge failed to appreciate or give due credit to the statistical studies carried out under Brinton's leadership. For one thing, Brinton demonstrated that only one of every four soldiers who had been wounded ever returned to full duty. His studies also showed that the fighting strength of the army lay in the prevention of sickness, particularly smallpox, malaria, and diarrhea. In an army of 2.2 million, the Union lost more than 275,000 to disease and discharged more than 220,000 from the service due to chronic disability.

In August 1864, after serving three years and four months, Major S. T. Trowbridge, Surgeon-in-Chief, 8th Reg. III Vol. Inf. 3rd Div. 17th Army Corps, received an honorable discharge. Returning to Decatur, he formed a partnership with his old friend, Dr. W. J. Chenoweth, and devoted himself to surgery. His reminiscences recount several difficult surgeries; his efforts to reorganize the county medical society, which ceased to exist during the war; and his communications to the Illinois Legislature to secure higher qualifications for practicing physicians. In 1868, Trowbridge was elected president of the Illinois State Medical Society and in that capacity spoke on behalf of the rights of women to become members of the medical profession. "The day is here," he said, "when women will do their part in all great literary and professional pursuits as they desire, and that we are very much in favor of their having that privilege." As for Trowbridge's partner, Dr. William J. Chenoweth remained active in the Illinois State Medical Society and in the District Medical Society of Central Illinois where he occasionally read papers and served as associate editor for the *Illinois Medical Recorder.*[5]

In March 1869, letters of nomination and recommendation were sent to President Grant and signed by Governor Richard J. Oglesby and U.S. Representatives Jesse Hale Moore, John A. Logan, Samuel W. Moulton, Norman Buel Judd, John F. Farnsworth, John Baldwin Hawley, Ebon C. Ingersoll, and Burton C. Cook supporting the appointment of Dr. Trowbridge as U.S. Consul.

Those places under consideration included San Juan, Santiago, Trinidad, Kingston, Nassau, Odessa, Singapore, Leeds, Manchester, Acapulco, Turles Island, and Honolulu.[6]

On April 19, 1869, Trowbridge was appointed by President Grant to be United States Consul for the port of Vera Cruz along the eastern coast of Mexico. His appointment came at a period of immense importance in that the forces of the puppet emperor Austrian Archduke Maximilian, who had attempted to establish an empire in Mexico, had just withdrawn. The earlier imposition of this ruler by Napoleon III, who hoped to provide France with markets and raw materials as well as halt Anglo-Saxon hegemony over Latin peoples through a French-protected empire, was short-lived. Neither Maximilian nor the French anticipated the resistance of the Mexican people or the resilience of the Union, which steadfastly withheld diplomatic recognition because of Maximilian's cooperation with the Confederacy. By 1865, Maximilian's French-made government was showing signs of collapse. Lew Wallace, the same general whom Trowbridge despised for his disobedience of Grant's orders at the battle of Shiloh, had patriotically raised money and supplies from friends in Indiana that he provided to the Mexican leader Benito Juárez to fight against Maximilian. The emperor was executed at Querétaro by the partisans on June 19, 1867.

Two years later, Trowbridge arrived in Vera Cruz, twelve days after his predecessor, Mr. E. H.

Saulnier, had died. General Rosecrans was then Envoy Extraordinary and Minister Plenipotentiary, soon to be replaced by the Hon. Thomas H. Nelson. Rosecrans had been an active promoter of American railroad interests in Mexico and increased American capital in the region by building ties between leading American investors and Mexican politicians.

Trowbridge's own commission was received by President Benito Juárez and his secretary of state, Sebastian Lerdo de Tijada. His work began on July 11, 1869. By the time he completed his assignment, Lerdo, the new president of Mexico, had become more cautious regarding the business interests of Mexico's northern neighbor.

At the time of Trowbridge's assignment, relations between the United States and Mexico were strained, with multiple claims having been lodged by citizens of each government against the other in the aftermath of the Civil War. Added to this was the presence of large numbers of Confederate ex-patriots who, following Lee's surrender, had sought to escape the humiliation of defeat by immigrating to Brazil, British Honduras, Cuba, Canada, Egypt, Jamaica, Japan, Mexico, Venezuela, and other countries. Eight to ten thousand Southerners had immigrated individually and in small groups to Latin America, most of them to Mexico. Maximilian had hoped that the ex-Confederates and their families would eventually provide a barrier of settlements in northern Mexico against possible American expansionism. The success of Major General Philip Sheridan and his army of fifty-two thousand troops in sealing the border with Mexico brought an end to Confederate emigration. For those, however, who did migrate, Trowbridge observed that these "disaffected secessionists, who would no longer live under the U. S. Flag . . . were by no means courteous to the representatives of our government." Among the exiles who stayed in Mexico were Texas Governor Pendleton Murrah, Louisiana Governor Henry Watkins Allen, and General Walter H. Stevens.[7]

While stationed in Vera Cruz, Trowbridge never forgot his medical roots and, being observant by nature, took time to study several cases of yellow fever whose treatment he questioned. Believing that the objective for the physician was to maintain the integrity of the mucous membranes that tended to break down under the disease, he recommended "a free purge" of castor oil followed by frequent doses of sulphite of soda, chlorate of potassa, and other disinfectant agents. These, along with hot foot-baths and fresh air constituted his recommended treatment.

The *Autobiography of Silas Thompson Trowbridge M.D.* ends in 1874 with the marriage of the consul's daughter, Ada, to a merchant of Vera Cruz, and a six-day family vacation trip on the Vera Cruz and Mexico Railroad to see the sights. Although the autobiography does not recount Trowbridge's later years, we know from U.S. State Department records and those of the American Medical Association that he remained in the diplomatic service from 1869 to 1882 and, upon retirement, moved to Napa, California, where he filed for a veteran's pension. He died in 1893 at the age of sixty-eight and is buried in Tulocay Cemetery in Napa County.

Readers will find pleasure in reading the *Autobiography of Silas Thompson Trowbridge M.D.* The author provides a fascinating look at the practice of medicine as well as the obvious interplay of medicine and politics in the years before, during, and after the Civil War.

—John S. Haller Jr., Professor of History
Southern Illinois University Carbondale

—Barbara Mason, Curator, The Pearson Museum
School of Medicine, Southern Illinois University

NOTES

1. John S. Haller, Jr., "Sampson of the Terebinthinates: Medical History of Turpentine," *Southern Medical Journal,* 77 (1984), 750–54.

2. John S. Haller, Jr., *Farmcarts to Fords: A History of the Military Ambulance, 1790–1925* (Carbondale: Southern Illinois University Press, 1992), 26–39.

3. Frank R. Freemon, *Gangrene and Glory: Medical Care During the American Civil War* (New Jersey: Associated University Presses, 1998), 145.

4. See John H. Brinton, *Personal Memoirs of John H. Brinton Civil War Surgeon, 1861–1865* (Carbondale: Southern Illinois University Press, 1996).

5. David J. Davis, *History of Medical Practice in*

Illinois. Vol. 2, *1850–1900* (Chicago: Illinois State Medical Society, 1955).

6. *Letters of Application and Recommendation During the Administration of Ulysses S. Grant, 1869–1877.* M968, Reel 62.

7. See Andrew F. Rolle, *The Lost Cause: The Confederate Exodus to Mexico* (Norman: University of Oklahoma Press, 1965); John Mason Hart, *Empire and Revolution: The Americans in Mexico since the Civil War* (Berkeley: University of California Press, 2002).

AUTOBIOGRAPHY

OF

SILAS THOMPSON TROWBRIDGE M. D.

LATE SURGEON OF THE 8. REG. ILL.VOL. INF.;
SURGEON IN CHIEF OF THE 3. DIVISION 17.
ARMY CORPS; PRESIDENT OF THE ILL-
INOIS STATE MEDICAL SOCIETY;
U. S. CONSUL AT VERACRUZ,
&c. &c. &c.

PRINTED
BY THE
FAMILY
OF THE
AUTHOR.

VERA CRUZ, 1872.

DEDICATED

To those who are most interested in this history, and whose criticisms will be the most rigid and yet charitable of all mankind: to those whose courteous walks in life has ever been my guide and good example: and who have ever exulted with modest pride in my successes, and cheered me on to better fortunes in my defeats. To my dearly beloved WIFE and darling CHILDREN: to whom my heart is consecrated as but poor reward for the love and happiness they have always bestowed upon me. To them this book is dedicated in greatful gratitude to God the giver of these perfect Gifts, praying for their earthly happiness and wellfare, and that the succeeding chapters of THIS LIFE may be more profitable to them and all my fellow mortals.

S. T. T.

PREFACE

The work of presenting these pages has been no inconsiderable one for me. The utility of it, I shall not attempt to defend. It was written wholly from memory as it lingers upon my mind, without the support of any notes or documents which I should have been pleased to have consulted; but of which aid I was debared, because all the notes, documents, letters and family traditions as are in existence, are thousands of miles distant from us; and the paroxysm of witing, and printing the same by the eager energy of young hands, assailed us by reason of the purchase, as a beneficent playihing for my children, of a small hand printing press; and the desire to have something in the printing line for them to do in which they might be interested.

It was thought that should a plain style of narration be adopted, that one event would be most likely to introduce another, and thus a chain of circumstances constituting the non-eventful and even tenor of an ordinary man's career might amuse and encourage the young members of his family to make theirs better and more profitable. This mode was attempted but so frepuently failed that the writer often threatened to place a preface of apology and excuse in the middle of the book in order to complete its homogeniousness.

I had expected to have rewritten and arranged in a succession of periods and chapters the whole work: but no sooner did the writing commence than busy little fingers furnished the "proof" of the same, and called for more "copy".

It was expected that the type setting enthusiasm would soon subside, and so it did: but not until the mould had cast the fashion; and so it must be followed.

Feeling assured that none but relatives and friends will ever read the following pages, and that by those he is conscious a gnerous criticism will be extended; and thus the work is submitted to those who have the fullest affections of

THE AUTHOR.

VERA CRUZ, 1872

AUTOBIOGRAPHY
OF
SILAS THOMPSON TROWBRIDGE M. D.

The subject of these pages was born on a farm in Harrison Township, Fayette County, Indiana, February 19. 1826. His Parents, LEVI and ABIGAIL Trowbridge, had emigrated from the state of New York, the year before, with a family of two daughters and four sons. They had lost two infant children (both boys,) before leaving New York. My sisters, Polly and Sally, were the oldest of the family; and then Billy Smith, Franklin Young, Samuel, John De Mott, (and his twin brother unnamed,) Edwin Nester, and last Silas Thompson, were the christian names and order of births of the family of which I sprang. My Father was born in Connecticut, January 16. 1783. He served his country as a Captain of Infantry in the army, which operated against the British forces in 1814, on the Cannadian frontier. He was married to Miss Abigail Smith, in the early years of his majority; and settled in central New York. In those days, and near the place of their residence. the Red Man of the Forest made his home. Therefore, a life of primitive simplicity and privation was theirs to follow; in which was mingled, as by the relentless force of fate, more of the rougher, than the smoother elements. Being of daring and enterprising natures; clothed with little of this worlds goods; and their numerous family, for whose interests and wellfare they had devoted themselves; with no better result than a good common school education for those old enough to receive it; they determined to settle in the "far west" of that day; and did so in the Fall of 1825. My Mother was the eldest of a large family; many members of which are still living in central Pennsylvania. My Grand Father Smith, was drummer boy in the Revolutionary War, and was one of the musicians who played Yankee Doodle, at the surrender of Lord Cornwallace. He was a Silver-smith by trade. My Mother was born in Vermont January 19. 1782. She was a devoted christian, of the Baptist persuasion; an indulgent, self-sacrifising, and doting Mother; a generous, just and hospitable neighbor; and in the fullest sense of the word, an eminently good and highly honored woman. She was my Father's safe counsellor; and supported him boldly and cheerfully in all his daring schemes and enterprises. But "death loves a shining mark:" and she died, at the old homestead in Fayette County Indiana, August 26. 1839. At this time the family consisted of my Father, my next older brother and myself. The other members being married, and settled in the immediate neighborhood, save Franklin, and Samuel, who had died several years before. Franklin had grown to man's estate, with more than ordinary promise of usefulness and talent; had made the profession of Medicine his employment and enlisted so much energy and labor in its arduous course that his exposures and toil ripened Tuberculosis; of which he died, at the place of his location; at Lebanon, Warren County Ohio, and in his 24. year. Samuel, died in infancy. The death of my Mother occasioned a breaking up of house-keeping for my Father; — my brother Edwin, going to live with our oldest brother, Billy; and I, with my brother-in-law, W. W. Thomas, who had married my oldest sister, Polly, and lived near by.— This move gave us the opportunity of going to the best school in that part of the State. I resided two years with my brother-in-law, going to school during the year, save in the season of corn planting and the raising thereof and through the harvesting of wheat, oats and hay; at

which time I "made a full hand," on my
Brother-in-law's farm. For these two years
I had most excellent opportunities, in teachers and associations, for learning and mental
culture ; and for which my mind has, at all
times since, been filled with gratitude and
thanks.

Soon after the death of my Mother, my
Father converted his limited means into
wild lands, and gave them to his three
youngest children, John, Edwin and Silas.
This consisted of 160 acres, in Clarke
County Missouri, to John ; 160 acres in
Madison County Indiana, to Edwin ; and
80 acres, in Bradford county Indiana, to me.
Although I received but 80 acres, yet, it
was considered equal in value to the others;
owing to its contiguity to the county seat.

At the age of sixteen I commenced
teaching, in a common district school ; in
the same district in which I was born, and
had taken my first days in schooling.

Like Ichobod Crane, of Sleepy Hollow,
I "boarded round," on this occasion; and
although I spent two thirds of the time with
Lester Ellis, my brother-in-law who lived
thereat, and one fourth more with warm
personal friends and patrons, Minor Meeker,
Joshua Weightman, and Lewis Ellis ; yet
the remnant of time not included in these

two thirds and one fourth, I spent "swinging round the circle" as President Johnson would say,

At this period of my life I suffered fearfully from the malady known as bashfulness. And overwhelming paroxysms of it would assail me when in the presence of any respectable person with whom I was not on the most intimate and almost confidential terms. So that the expression of "boarding round" has yet to me a most significant and impressive sound, although, I can truly say that the disease has not oppressed me since 20 years ago.

I followed the employment of teaching during the winter season for several years. In all this time of teaching I progressed more rapidly in learning than ever before. I would highly recommend that the young, after sufficient preparation, should become teachers, and throw all their energies into those schmes which embellish the minds of others. It is like Shakespeare's mercy; "it is twice blessed; it blesseth him that receives, and he that gives." And to plant those seeds on the rich soil of life's young dreams, is garnering stores for Heaven.

During the winter of 1842 and 1843 I traveled with my father from Indiana to the interior parts of the states of New York

and Pennsylvania selling horses. This was
an historically severe winter; and the one in
which I became 17 years of age. Then it
was that I first saw my two Grand Mothers,
respectively in their 93. and 95. year of age.
Grand Mother Trowbridge, or James, rather
for she had married after the death of my
Grand father, was verry frail; and time had
robbed her of most of the faculties of the
five senses. But with her, an exceedingly
interesting result of habit lingered to great
perfection. Although she was almost blind,
yet, she could knit "ribbed" stockings with
wonderful accuracy: but could not remember
where her knitting was, if it were out of her
hand but for a moment, although she never
put it in any other than a certain fixed place,
and in a particular order. The explanation
for this peculiarity is found in the fact that
she had recently moved, with her son,into a
new house; which act of moving she could
not remember and always thought herself in
her old home; but would learn, with well
marked emotions of astonishment and surprise, many times each day, of her change
of habitation. The new chimney corner was
not the old one to her; and the ancient care-
worn brain could only retain a recollection
of where she should put aside her work,
but not where to find it. Our modern habits

and machinery has so changed domestic
employment, that I deem it just to explain
this knitting feat, of which I have spoken.
To knit ribs, with regularity and with the
common knitting needle, requires a crtain
number of stitches taken, say for example
5 stitches; then the needles are so changed
as to throw the the next 5 stitches with the
"wrong side out," and creating an offset in
fabric. These alternations of certain numbers
of stitches constitute the ribs, but require
constant accuracy in the count, in order to
be perfect. And although her age and infirm-
ities had robbed her of memory and sight
to almost the last degree, yet she always
produced the "ribs" in symmetrical perfection. She lived but a year after this, dying
in her 96. year.

My Grand Mother Smith sustained her
great age with all her faculties bright and
her disposition as gay and cheerful as in
her prime of life. Her second sight was
quite good; and her amiable qualities always
predominent, drew around her an admiring
multitude, mostly those in whom her own
blood descended. She recollected with perfect clearness and accuracy the tragic history
of the Revolutionary War; having learned
it from observation in the sad school of its
transaction. But it was allotted for her to

live but a few years longer; dying in her
96. year, most highly honored and respected
by a numerous chain of kindred and friends.

This winter's work of horse selling and
kindred visiting was a severe one on me.
It was intensely cold and in some of our
excursions I contracted a violint "cold"with
a slight influenza which conbination, just at
the age in which my voice was undergoing those mutations observable between
youth and manhood, so spoiled it that it
was with dificulty that I could speak in
such a manner as to be understood. I chose
a very healthy alternative and did but little
talking. I am much impressed with the belief that reticence, as a rule, is a surer stepping stone to popularity than garrolity.

Returning in the Spring to Indiana, I
had an opportunity, while in transit, to visit
the site of some of the military achievements
of my father in the "Late War" with England. Also at the same time, and near by,
we visited the Falls of Niagara. These were
great and valuable days to me. Days which,
in after times, fed my mind with aims and
aspirations for patriotic devotion on the
one hand; and of grandeur and sublimity
in the contemplation of the works of God
on the other. However little these personal
influences have affected others; yet they

were frequent topics of thought and resolve on my part;and therefore worthy of mention in this place. In the fall of 1843, I, with my Father, accompanied my Brother John, to Mc Lean County Illinois, whence John had moved with his family the year before, and had returned on business to the old home in Indiana. Arriving in Illinois in November, I at once offered my services as school teacher and was engaged in a country district near a place now known as Heyworth on the Illinois Central Rail Road. Here I first became acquainted with Mr. Harrison Noble, at that time County Surveyor of Mc. Lean county. In this acquaintance I was extremely fortunate. For soon we became intimate, and our natures were so allied to each other that until the death of Dr Harrison Noble in 1870, that intimacy and fervent friendship continued with no diminution or interruption. It was he who induced the late Doctor Stephen W. Noble and myself to study medicine. We commenced this enterprise in the winter of 1845 and 1846, reading at the farm residence of Mr. Joseph Noble, the father of S. W. Noble. The latter, was a young gentleman of my own age; and a schollar in the school I was then teaching. The following Spring of 1846, I taught a three months term receiving therefor, wheat at thirty seven cents per bushel; which I transported to Chicago in wagons, a distance of 130 miles or more—there not being a foot of rail-road in the state at that time.—

I commenced the study of medicine simply as a pastime and a pleasure; not desiring to become a practitioner. My father, learning of my progress in the study, entertained fears that I might become fascinated by its promises and thereby induced to embark in the practice; requested me to turn my attention to some other literary field; feeling a preference for the profession of Law. He encouraged the idea of returning to Indiana, whither in June 1846. I went, making my home again with my estimable and worthy brother-in-law, Mr. William W. Thomas. On leaving Illinois on this occasion I saw, at Urbana Champaign county Illinois, for the last time my venerable Father. In the Fall of this year he was attacked by a continued form of fever, which carried him off.

On arriving in Indiana I had an opportunity of exchanging my 80 acres of Blackford land with my oldest brother for some 13 shares of stock in the White Water Vally Canal Company. This, at the time was considered a good exchange; but a year developed facts forcibly convincing me that it was not. For twice within that year the said canal was well nigh washed from the face of the earth by unprecedented high water in the White Water river, along which the canal was built. I felt this loss severely in as much as it disturbed the foundation of all my "real estate" and some of my designes in life. This casuality thoroughly illustrated to my comprehension the fact, that

"The best laid schemes of men and mice
Oft gang a glee."

With no better employment than teaching by which to redeem my deluged stock and gain an independent living, I continued that employment one term longer.

During the Fall of 1847 my next older brother, Edwin, who was likewise a teacher and myself formed a copartnership and purchased such chemical aparatus as was wanted to illustrate those more brilliant chemical formula, a working model of the then new and novel invention of the magnetic Telegraph, and such other popular and scientific devices as in our judgement would meet the public eye with favor, and set out upon a tour of popular lectures. My brother did the lecturing, while my chosen duty was billposter, door-keeper and general assistant. Although his eloquence far surpassed my expectations, and my door-keeping and assistance was as complete as could be made, yet, it was a financial failure; and we therefore, soon abandoned the business.

These financial defeats determined me to renew the study of medicine with the fixed intention of making it my labor of life. Therefore, Edwin and I dissolved partnership in the show business; there falling to me, by mutual consent, the chemical fixtures and Edwin took the wagon; and returned to Indiana, where he soon married Miss Susan Carver, and settled down to be an industrious and well respected farmer.

Our peregrinations had come to a close at Le Roy, Illinois, at which place our brother John resided. On the 24. day of February 1848 I vigorously and determinedly recommenced reading medicine with Dr. David Cheney of that place. I was errand boy and wood chopper for the little hotel and boarding house which my brother kept; doing this for my board and exercise, and at the same time reading for a daily task 75 pages of medical literature for every day of the week. My former companions, Harrison and Stephen Noble had pushed rapidly into the mysteries of the healing art and graduated at the Ohio Medical College in the Spring of 1848. They came home with their Diplomas; and Harrison opened an office at

his former residence; and Stephen came to
locate at the little village of Le Roy, where
I was then residing. They rapidly became
distinguished in the profession, because of
their success and their many high and worthy qualities. I had the honor in subsequent
years of proposing their names to the Illinois State Medical Society for the high and
honorable office of President of that Society;
and also the satisfaction of seeing their zeal
and professional accomplishments rewarded
by being unanimously elected. Dr H. Noble
was elected in 1855 at Vandalia and Dr. S.
W. Noble in 1867 at Bloomington.

I pursued the study of medicine from
the time of my recommencement until I became a graduate, with but one slight interruption which was for a two months tour of
cattle driving for the Hon. W. H. Cheney,
and for the purpose of replenishing my
exhausted pocket money. This was in the
Summer of 1848; and the net proceeds of
that enterprise was $ 31.00 which was suffi-
cient for my necessities until I determined
to locate and practice medicine some time
afterwards. After returning from Indiana
through which state I had followed a drove
of 250 head of fat cattle belonging to Mr.
Cheney, I removed from Le Roy to Ran-
dolph's Grove, and lived in the family of Dr.

Harrison Noble, reading and riding with him to see all his interesting cases. We became good practical chemists during the winter on a very small outlay of money. With about $25 invested in glass tubes, rods, retorts sand-baths and reagents, we illustrated Turner's Inorganic Chemistry complete, save the manufacture of Strychnia and and Sulphuric Acid, which required specific and expensive machinery. We made a strong Galvanic Battery, Electrical machine, sand baths, stands, transfer tubs, gasometers, &c, beside reading our appointed task of 75 pages a day. Early in my readiug I laid down a rule, and denominated it a "cast iron rule;" that I would not pass a word in reading of which I could not give its deffinition and root. This caused me very much hard work of dictionary search, and drew heavily upon my time allotted to the day's work of 75 pages. This was extra to that day's work; but the chemical reading was a part of it.

The year and more which I spent in reading to this task of 75 pages per day was the severest scholastic training I ever did. For me, it was almost impossible to accomplish the daily work and sit in a chair by a desk or table. And to hold the book, weighing from 5 to 8 pounds, while either sitting, standing or walking, would have been out of the question entirely. The most efficient mode of reading, or easiest position I could assume, was one which, although very satisfactory to me, has never been adopted by any of the hard students who have studied under me. It was by sitting upon the floor against the wall with a triangular block for my feet to rest upon, with the book resting on my lap just at the right distance for reading, and a medical dictionary upon one side and Webster's dictionary upon the other, and paper and pencil in the book I was reading for notes, that I could accomplish my task with the greatest ease. Thus equipped I could sit for 3 hours and capture 25 pages, when I would take working exercise for an hour, and then be ready for another 3 hour sitting, if it should require so much time to master the 25 pages; then exercise again, and so finish the day by another sitting for the final 25 pages. I have given this ritual of a day as illustrative of all, for a period of near 14 months thus spent, when my finances demanded a change, and I determined to locate and offer my services to the public as a physician. In taking this determination I was supported by the advice of my companions, the Drs Noble, who argued my competence from the amount of labor I had accomplished, and the test cases in practice I had seen. In the usual course of medical studentage, from 8 to 25 pages per day has been considered as much as the student could well digest, and from 3 to 5 years thus drawn out had offered, as a rule, a set of lazy physicians which, without the aid of lectures and clinics, would have been a positive sourse of danger in place of a blessing to any commúnity in which they may have located.

The amount of reading comprehended in the 14 months was equal, if not greater, in the aggregate, than the general average of students at the end of 5 years. The only question then to settle was; had I comprehended the subject matter of my reading? Taking it for granted, with my conscience considerably tilted akimbo, I resolved to seek a location and "swing my shingle" as a physician I therefore left the office and practice of Dr. H. Noble, and went to Indiana, where, in a short time I was enabled to exchange my 13 hundred dollars of canal stock for an old buggy and less than a hundred dollars worth of medicines, books and instruments which I put into the buggy and again returned to Illinois. After prospecting a short time I finally concluded to stick my stake of location at the farm of Mr. Harvey

Turner, near New Castle, Logan County, Illinois. The place is now known as Atlanta, on the St Louis & Chicago R. R.. I arrived at Mr. Turner's farm ready for service, July 4. 1849. I was a little over 23 years of age, beardless and very verdant in appearance, and the next approaching three months, were the healthiest known in many years, before. The citizens were an enterprising, intelligent and social set of farmer families; and I was unusually well received among them; with many voluntary promises of patronage, when the sad days of affliction should come in which a physician would be required. For my board and loundry service and full provision for my horse, I contracted to pay Mr. Turner $ 1.50 per week; and at the close of three months, I found my practice exactly paid my board bill.

In all my first cases, my great fears were, that I should make mistakes in diagnosis; or, in determining what was the true disease. And to sharpen my apprehesions and distrust I diagnosticated an ordinary remittent fever, with high bounding pulse, and agonizing headach, as a severe attack of Inflammation of the brain; and bled my patient profusely; gave him antiphlogistic remedies, and promised to see him again. I did so, and many sympathysing friends principally the more aged female members of the neighborhood had anticipated my visit, and out of interest and curiosity, remained until after I should make my call. I was astonished at the numbers I met, and construed the visitation to portend no good to me; and supposed my patient much worse. But fate had ordered it different. My patient was so much better that the suspicion flashed across my mind, that it was a case of Intermittent, or Remittent fever and not inflammation of the brain as I had previously thought. His recovery was rapid, and my name well started in the neighborhood.

This was my second case. The first, being one of a young man who was bitten by a Rattle snake, also giving me good report. With these cases and the good favor of the people, who very much desired a physician in the locality, my way was well promised; although my amiable hostess constantly said that "he does not look like a doctor." But still, she was my friend and gave me both employment and recommendation. Yet her ideal "doctor" should have the reverential grey hair and sober demeanor of aristocracy. No wonder my unpretentious personale did not fill the bill of her ideal Medicus. This three months reidence at New Castle convinced me that it was not a good location for one wanting much practic, as it was evidently a healthy location, and too closely surrounded with other medical gentlemen of well established reputation, for me to force my way beyond my immediate neighborhood. I therefore consulted with the Drs. Noble and concluded to seek a field elsewhere.

A short search for a location determined me to stick my stake at Decatur, the county seat of Macon County Illinois, whither I went, arriving there Occber 28. 1849, with $3. 25 in my pockets. $3. 00 of which I paid to have my drugs and effects brought after me. In those primitive days in Illinois, board, and the usual living expenses were very light; for money was scarce and valuable in proportion to what it is at present.

Decatur was small, though quite old, especislly in appearance, containing not more than 600 to 700 inhabitants. There was no other town within 25 miles of it, and but two doctors in the place to do service over an area of territory considerably over 25 miles in diameter. It was thinly settled, only in a belting of farms on prairies skirting the timber.

On arriving in Decatur I formed the acquaintance of one of the best lawyers of the place, Captain J. S. Post, who introduced me to the two medical gentlemen

then, and still living there, Dr. Joseph King,
and Dr. Tho's H. Read, and to many other
of the most prominent and influential gentlemen of the village. He kindly offered me
his office to occupy in common with himself;
and was always afterwards rendering me
many kind offices and attentions. The assiduous friendship of Captain Post, constant
through all the various circumstances which
came up to test it, is one of the happiest
recollections of my life.

A few days after being introduced to
Dr. King, I offered to take any of his long,
dark, hot, cold, muddy or worthless rides
off his hands, and do the best I could for
his patients, and report the fees, cases and
treatment in full to him on returning; stating
that it was experience that I wanted and I
could not expect to obtain practice unless I
was endorsed by favorable results.

Dr. King was doing nine tenths of all
the business there; was a first class gentleman; a good physician; and possessed the
entire confidence of the community. He was
an eminently practical physician; a good and
close observer; and naturally a man of fine
sense and judgement.

Dr. Read was quite old; and, being a
cripple from birth, desired the ease and
quiet of a christian retirement. He had never

at any period of his life probably, entertained
very high aspirations for practice. However,
he had lived in the place for many years,
being the first physician to locate there, and
had called round him a small circle of con-
fiding patrons who gave him their unwaver-
ing support. Dr. Read is a gentleman of the
old school; eminently a good and honorable
man.

Neither of these gentlemen were grad-
uates of any medical college; yet they were
not defective in the practical knowledge of
the healing art; and Dr. King had attended
medical lectures at the Ohio Medical College
when the great Eberle was associated in the
faculty. My professional intercourse with
them was regulated by the most rigid rules
of medical etiquette and by them as rigidly
reciprocated. Therefore we never had mis-
understandings nor ought but harmony and
friendship in all our long acquaintance.

Both these gentlemen were wealthy, so
to say, in comparison to their neighbors;
both rather inclined to take the world easy,
and hence my proposition to Dr. King to do
some of his hard work for him, arrested his
attention and he soon sent me a case. Not
however, until he had thoroughly sounded
me over cases which he had been kind
enough to show me.

My first case was a circumstance. A child was accidentally scalded on the scalp by its mother; Dr. Read being called to its relief, applied tincture of Opium and directed that the parts should be excluded from the air; when seeing the injury was but slight, went home. The alcohol of the medicine irritated the scald more than the opium soothed, and the exclusion of air not being attended to, as directed, it was but natural that the little fellow should yell horribly, and frighten an already self-reproaching mother. She was one of the class who are curious to try the last new doctor, and hence I was called. I went very promptly, not knowing that Dr. Read had been there, and applied "Caron Oil," with the effect of quieting the child to sleep in less than five minutes time from its first application. I did not know for a long time afterwards that this was Dr. Read's case; and when I learned it, I apologized to him for my unintentio al intrusion; but the woman had so publicly abused him that the apology was very coldly received.

In the cases sent me by Dr. King I rendered careful treatment and very prompt attention, and was cautious to do full justice to the Doctor. He, like the great Webster, was very fond of fishing; and Mr. Berg would rate him high in his Society for the Prevention of Cruelty to Animals, because of his compassion manifested to "old Rock", as it would consume the better part of a day for him to execute a drive of 5 miles and return. These tardy habits gave him the name of being careless; against which unjust aspersion I always defended him with much care. He soon became my warm friend and did me many kind services.

For one year I thus pushed forward in the department of practice as rapidly as opportunity offered, accomplishing for the time a book and cash account of $336. 00, which was by no means equal to that many dollars in hand.

To me the name of surgeon had a musical sound; and my study and research ran largely in that direction. An incident in this year's practice shows how insignificant events sometimes contrl a medical reputation. My frend, Dr. King, was called to visit a case which he had been attending for more than a year. It was one of a bright little girl afflicted with a rotting of the bone of the thigh. (Necrosis.) The doctor, knowing my predilection for surgery, and feeling a thorough repugnance for every branch of it, asked me to visit the case for him; telling the father that if I thought I could assist the child by an operation, that he should have me make arrangements for it; and that I should be considered as the principal in the case. I went, a distance of 16 miles, and in the examination with strong forceps, I detached the rotton portion from the scarf bone which had been formed round it and from the sound bone of the thigh. Discovering the true state of affairs; and by a slight enlargement of the apperture whence pus and small fragments of bone had been escaping, say to an inch or more, I was enabled to remove the whole of the diseased portion. It was an easy matter to show the parents that this was the offending substance, and in as much as it comprised at least two thirds of the entire thigh bone, I predicted that it would, without further interference, result in a radical recovery with full usefullness and symetry of limb. The prognosis was verified; and in that neighborhood my name and conduct were well canvassed, and many marvellous additions made to it which no one could maintain short of a realization of the powers of inspiration. The father of this little patient learned by some means unknown to me; that I was a seventh son, with no intervening daughters, and therefore a "natural doctor." I always accused Dr. King or Captain Post of perpetrating this hoax upon the credulity of a superstitious community. There is no field of intelligent employment wherein a people of sound sense and judgement are so easily led into extravagant notions of absurdities and foolishness as in the domain of medicine. My nature revolted against any such an idea as a supernatural agency; and I felt that my hard days of toil and common sense were slandered by what was thoughtlessly ascribed to be a natural excellence.

Early in life I had imbibed a profound regard for the Order of Free Masonry. My father and brother-in-law, Mr. Thomas, were Royal Arch Masons; and I often promised myself the preferment of a membership should my personal worth and acceptability entitle me to such. Therefore on the fifth of May 1850, after my application was accepted, I was made an Entered Apprentice Mason in due form, in Macou Lodge No. 8, at Decatur, Illinois. Here I met a band of good men, who were worthy of the Order; and with whom my association and membership was, for many years, most agreeable. Before the 24. of June of that year, I was raised to the degree of a Master Mason; and having but little else to do, I entered with great relish and enthusiasm into the work, and soon became a "bright" member.

In 1855 a Chapter of Royal Arch Masons was established in Decatur; and I was one of the first three persons "exalted" to the Royal Arch degree in MACON CHAPTER No. 21. This was in the Spring; and in June following, I was elected High Priest of the Chapter. At the convocation of the Grand Chapter of the state at Jacksonville, in the succeeding September, I was elected Grand Scribe. The following year, at Springfield, I was chosen Grand King. These convocations came off in the season of my busiest practice; and I found it incompatible with my interests to accept masonic offices longer. The office of Grand King of the Grand Chapter of Illinois in 1856 entitled me to membership, by delegation, in the General Grand Chapter of the United States; which, in that year held its session at Hartford Connecticut. But not being inclined to leave my practice I deputized my worthy Companion M. J. Noyes, P. G. H. P. to fill my place; and ever after left the official management of masonry to other hands.

In the latter part of October 1850, I borrowed $100 of Samuel Rea, and on the 28. of that month, left Decatur to attend a course of medical lectures at Rush Medical College of Chicago. Arriving there, I at once matriculated in full, and was directed by Professor N. S. Davis to a certain house where he felt assured good rooms and fare could be obtained. On inquiring there, the lady informed me that her rooms were all taken; but that there was living just opposite to her a young widow who had the very class of accommodation I had described; and that it was thought that she might be induced to take boarders. Accordingly I at once called upon her and asked for board and was, after a short consultation with her parents, admitted as such, at the residence of Mrs. Emeline Henderson. Here, again, hard work presented itself and was accomplished with a full determination to graduate that term of lectures. I matriculated as a practitoner and placed my name on all the quiz lists of the professors in order that they might well know of my qualifications. Being blessed with good health it was an easy labor, though it required constant application, to keep up well and bright with the lecture course. The result was that I graduated that term without dificulty, receiving an unanimous vote of the faculty. I wrote my THESIS of 20 pages, according to the rule required, and one of similar length for a fellow student; who, in order to keep well up with the course had to devote his entire time to the lectures and his books.

The winter of 1850 and '51 was an exceedingly interesting one to me. Strong resolves had been formed of accomplishing all my faculties could command in the way of the consumption of medical facts; and had denied myself every liberty of recreation or amusement which might compromise a single item of information or a moment of time by which it might be obtained. We saw that the appartments of our fair hostess would accommodate 5 or 6 more students as boarders, and she delegated me to select them. We were fortunate in gathering there good men and anxious students as companions; but each endowed with rare peculiarities. We had a white-livered nervous musician, a burley brusk irishman, a red headed mathematical yankee, a round red faced highlander, a sharp shrude fun making yarn spinning sucker, and myself to constitute the crowd at our "Social Hall." Add to these, the graces of our accomplished hostess and her female companions, and you have a picture of the elements of independent diversified society in a nutshell. I have often since thought that our "mess" could, through natural spectacles, observe a medical subject in as many different points and attitudes as it ordinarily possessed. It was a mutual agreement that our discussions should take the widest range that gentlity and courtesy permitted, and all assertions had to be backed by acceptable authority. It is an old observation that unlikes attract each other; and I believed this bevy of characteristic dissimilarities could live in diversified harmony for a four months campaign as profitably as any. The conjecture proved to be correct; for our sojourn was very harmonious and successful. We lived like lords of the manor: in fact, our generous hostess fed us upon the fattest of the markts and charged us so little for it that the hard work she was having done was costing much more than the weekly payments we had contracted to give her. I surmised as much, and proposed to the boarders to ascertain the facts in the case and report them. Finding it to be so; we offered to rent such furniture and rooms as we wanted, and let her withdraw from the house. This negociation being effected, we thereafter fared well enough, but quite different in quality and cheer from our former good entertainment.

Every member of our mess graduated that term of lectures, except two, who did not apply.

Our hostess, possessing fine musical talents, which with her many social qualities had clustered around her a large circle of admiring female friends, whose amiable and congenial natures and musical accomlishments were sufficient to subtract the attention and break the resolution of persons of far less susceptible natures than mine; especially when those resolutions were made for hard work and personal abnegation. For the first month my evenings were spent in the dissecting rooms mostly, and often in those chambers of the dead when there was but one companion to assist me would we pass the time until after midnight. The next morning lectures commenced at 8 A. M. and 4 of them of one hour each was listened to before noon, when we had an hour's recess, and then 4 more lectures of equal length in the after half of the day.

Chicago at that time contained only 28000 inhabitants; and the medical students were the terror of the town. Their recklessness and dare-devil dispositions had become proverbial: although I am firmly of the opinion that many mischief makers outside of the college did much to annoy a peaceable people which were never executed by the students, but for which they always had full credit. An example of this occured to my room mate and myself when we were walking one day; at which time we saw a

nicely dressed lady with a pretty little child
at her side who was annoying her very much
by stopping to pick up bright pieces of boxes
and papers and such things as appeared
beautiful to the little fellow, when she, on
looking back, discoverd us; and recognizing
us as medical students, said to her child
"come along! here comes some students;"
when it clung to its mother with well marked
expressions of alarm, and by no means thereafter hindered her progress. That child had
reflected upon us our standing from association in that society.

After Mrs. Henderson left us in the possession of her house we arranged, by well
defined bachelor's rules, our mode of living;
and our opportunities for study was, if not
so elegant, less frequently interrupted by
those sallies of wit and sentiment with which
we were so frequently assailed by herself
and companions previously. This change in
our boarding house occurred about two
months after the commencement of the college course. Socially we felt the loss of the
society of Mrs. Henderson pointedly, but
doubtless our progress in the medical sciencies was somewhat advanced by the change;
although, on my part, often calls at her
Father's residence whither she had moved,
compensated for the absence. It was with

no small degree of satisfaction on my part
that I was enabled to observe that those
calls were well received. Her society was
very attractive to me, and when I saw that
she in succession rejected the offers of one
of the most influential and extensive dry-
goods merchants, a well to do and handsome
Scotch grocer and provision merchant, an
exceedingly enthusiastic and volatile music
master, and her methodist preacher, and still
appeared flattered by the attentions I gave
her, it must be confessed that it made strong
war upon my lessons in medicine, although
it may have improved my ideas of belles-
lettres and the collateral sciencies of adorn-
ment. Thus passed the time in the huge
contest for a diploma and the thralldom of
love, until on the morning of the 11. of Feb.
1851, when an exciting crisis in those exciting times, turned up. Dr. Herrick, Professor
of anatomy, came in the amphitheatre of
the college to deliver his hour's lecture,
bearing a paper in his hand from which
he read a list of 6 names including mine,
and said that "those gentlemen would please
call at his office at 8 o-clock P. M. for the
purpose of attending to the ordinances of
the Green Room." One not situated as I was,
can hardly appreciate the shock which that
announcement gave me: for that hour was the

identicle one that had been settled upon by
Mrs. Henderson and myself, to be made one
in the bands of matrimony. It was intended
that the wedding should be of a private character with but a few friends to attend it and
no display. Those friends were of course
before this time invited, licence obtained,
her favorite though rejected, Methodist
priest engaged to administer the marriage
ceremony, and all things prepared for the
ordinance to take place. Immediatly after
reading this list of "doomed men" as the students called us, the professor launched forth
into the mysteries of Anatomy or at all events
he said something contiually for a long long
hour which of course was anatomy and good
anatomy too but no anatomical fact lodged
on my brain that day. Here was a predica-
ment. Here was a fix. I did not want the
Professors to know of the wedding, for fear
they might consistently conjecture that I
had been worshiping at the shrine of Venus
more than that of Esculapius. I was anxious
to be tried exactly on my merits and without
any prejudices. To beg off from the examination on the score of being previously engaged on any business would be to say to the
Professor that his labors and profession were
secondary articles of consideration to me and
the tests of his Green Room might be un-

pleasant, But something had to be done—
some compromise to be established.—Accordingly I delegated my friend and room
mate Dr. E.J.Rice a special committee of
investigation and conference fully instructed
to say to Dr.Herrick that "one of his class
included in his call for examination this
night, not expecting to be required before
your honor; has engaged to be married at
the same hour you appointed that he should
meet you. And fully believeing in the well
established phylosophical law of Impenetra-
bility, which says that no two objects can
occupy the same space at the same time; so
the law of Divisibility is incompatible with
vitality, and therefore the said unmentioned
student after sending his most gracious compliments to Professor Herrick, begs to say
in his judgement, it will be impossible to appear at both of those important appointments at the same time. And that he would
like to hold the collision of arms in an ar-
mistice until amicable terms of settlement
could be established." Accordingly our big
hearted and sensible Professor proposed to
meet us at 6 o-clock and examine us one
hour and that we could put off the marriage
ceremony "and after a vigorous exercise in
the Green Room he will be in an excellent
fix to hand over to a beautiful bride through

the instrumentality of a Methodist Minister."
Accordingly I informed Mrs. Henderson
that it was impossible for us to be married
at 8 o-clock and therefore it was agreed that
the hour should be delayed until 9 o-clock.
Six o-clock arrived and we were six anxious candidates seated at the office of Dr.
Herrick. The Dr. had presumed that the
bride-groom would not come to his examination, in as much as he had said that if the
delay of an hour was not acceptable to the
party, he would examine the gentleman at
another time. But I prefered to go then
and when Dr. Herrick met us, he smilingly
said that he "presumed one of his class was
in better business than attending on the ordinances of the Green Room." When an exceedingly well dressed member of the class
said "no Dr. he is here." Dr. H. looked quis-
ically at him and said "Ah! it is well." Evidently thinking that the bride-groom had
spoken for himself. It was so permitted to
pass and the examination began. I sat at
the foot of the class, or farthest from Dr.
Herrick, and next above me was S. L. Craig,
and next to him was Martin, the well dressed
gentleman. Those two students were illy prepared to encounter the questions propound-
ed and suffered all grades of mortfication,
not even answering correctly a single ques-

tion though they were very simple; and the
same easy questions would come to me and
were answered. The other members of the
class receiving abstruce test questions and
I answering Craig and Martin's easy ones
was rare fun for me; until one of the others
feeling that my task was too smooth said to
Dr. Herrick as it became my time to anwer,
"Dr.Herrick, Trowbridge is the one to put
through; he it is who is to be married to
night." The Professor and class laughed
heartily at the turn of affairs, and during the
remainder of the examinaton I had no more
of the cast off questions of Craig and Martin.
But all things must have an end and soon
this examination closed. We were married:
and on the 20. of Febuary 1851, I took my
diploma as Doctor of Medicine. Knowing
that the College term would close on that
date, and wishing to leave for Decatur as
soon there-after as possible, I had much to
do in a short time and hence the business
feature in our marriage before graduation.
The business affairs of Mr. Henderson had
been left by him at his death, some two and a
half years before, in an unsettled state and
the little that was left was near being lost by
the fore-closure of a mortgage and the expir-
ation of the time of redemption. Out of the
effects of the property there was 1200 dollars

in cash saved, on which we commenced the
offices of house-keeping in the little city of
Decatur, whither we arrived after an exceedingly arduous journey of 5 days. We had 40
miles by rail, 40 more by stage in which distance we tipped over twice, once severely
bruising Mrs. Trowbridge's head, but at
which time I saved her band-box and fine
bonnet by a master feat of paying full attention to the bonnet, and letting Mrs. Trowbridge take care of herself: for which devoted
act of galantry I received the first frown.
This occurred in the middle of night in a
dark and muddy wood and I was sure she
was out of patience with the driver. Then we
took the "Ocean Wave" Steam-boat and
sailed down the Illinois River from Aurora
to Beards-town, and rail again to Springfield,
then two days in a "coach and 4" to Decatur.
It was so muddy that even then with no one
in the coach but Mrs. Trowbridge, myself,
three trunks, and the aforesaid band-box
we "stuck" fast in the mud in the corporation
of Springfield. Immediately on arriveing at
Decatur I again embarked in practice and
had the good fortune to get a very respectable amount of it and at no time after that
as long as I lived in that city did I want for
patronage. The promptness with which I
attended to buisness gave me very many of

Dr.King's patients and during the months of
August, September and October, Dr. King
fell sick and then all his patients became
mine. During Spring much rainy weather
prevailed and the streams were high, and
this gave place to a long continued drouth
with much heat. As a consequence there
was a great amount of sickness mostly of
Intermittent and Remittent fevers, Conjestive
Chills and Dysintary. This year I did a harder
practice than at any other period of my life.
I often rode a circuit of 45 miles and visited
as high as 36 patients in as many as 13 different houses. Of course nearly the whole
24 hours would be occupied in those tedious
rides and but little sleep could be indulged
in. In the midst of this rush of practice I
ran short of Quinine and all its substitutes and
sent to Springfield, Chicago and St Louis
for more and our orders came back not filled
because the stocks were exhausted. A Druggist of our town said he knew he had some
in Springfield en route to Decatur from Cincinnati—then the best way of sending— but
that the drugs would not be in Decatur for
a week at best. I had some patients whose
lives were highly jeopardized every hour for
the want of it, and therefore proposed to the
said Druggist to go to Springfield armed with
an order from him to the freight master and

ransack his drug boxes for the wanted article. I made the trip to Springfield and return in 16 hours a distance of 80 miles. Of this 16 hours I rested my horse 3 hours in searching the drug boxes. I bought all the Quinine the Druggist had, at 13 dollars an oz, and had the pleasure of seeing all my cases recover who was then ill for want of it.*

It was in this year, November 27. 1851 that our first child was born. He was a sprightly fine boy, and our happiness at the gift of God was closely bordering adoration.

He grew in strength and beauty and was the perfect idol of my family, which then consisted of my own and Mr. Rockwell's. We had named him Lewis Edwin, after my brother; and a friend, Dr, John Lewis. During his year of dentition he contracted whooping cough and Cholera Infantum which reduced him very much and on the evening of the first of October 1852 he took a Remittant fever with a severe convulsion which was repeated on the morning of the 2. with fatal result. I cannot describe the dessolation of our home on this sad event. And now that

* Being the frail member of my father's family, I have every reason to rejoice at the rebound of constitutional forces which enabled me to accomplish the arduous labors. And in connection with this expression I hope I may be pardoned for the egotistical bearing of the following statement, In the athletic sports of running and jumping I was, this year, in my zenith of capability. As an instance, I jumped at one leap, on level ground, after running a few steps to gain momentum, twenty two feet and eight inches. A record of this feat was made on the Macon County books of Record by Mr. Samuel Rea, County Recorder, who witnessed and measured the jump.

we look at six children liveing with parental pride and fondness; yet, we cannot but feel how full our cup of happiness would now be, were it so decreed that our first gift could have been spared to head this blessed flock.

A new candidate for practice entered the field and claimed favors as a practitioner, with a wide spread of display in antecedents and credentials. He was a stump orator of no mean force, and soon saw that my castle must be leveled first and so directed his artillery at me and ridiculed the idea of a "boy Doctor" and of any sensible people endangering their lives in his hands. He did me but little harm however, and soon became a patient of the "boy Doctor" himself, and ever after that gave me ample justice. There was no physician permanently located at Decatur who desired to treat surgical cases and I was soon in the full possession of the field with more surgical instruments and appurtenances than was required for the cases which came to me to treat. I had several very important cases which resulted much to my credit and in subsequent years did much to maintain my position as chief surgeon of the place.

On the tenth day of August 1853. our home was made happy by the birth of our second child, which we named Ada Bell.

She was as beautifull and perfect as the hearts of parents could pray for; and grew in health and interest until her second summer when she took Cholera Infantum and all my fears were arroused lest we might loose her also; but cold weather came to her relief in time to save her life; although she was in iminent danger from the horrid climate of an Illinois summer.

The winter of 1853, produced many cases fo a very malignant form of Typhoid Pneumonia and by its ravages I lost six very prominent citizens out of 43 cases. Those 6 deaths did me great injury. I lost the patronage of many leading families thereby and although in my concience as I survey it at a distance of 18 years; in which, much experience has ripened a judgement; I am as proud of the achievement of seeing the 37 recoveries of that dreadfull and fatal malady, as I am of any medical service I ever rendered. But it is the pronounced judgement of fate, that a medical man shall not go upon his true merit. And as an instance of this appearantly sweeping assertion, I will here say that I have been accredited by some as possessing almost inspired powers; when my popularity was gained in cases over which my skill had little controll or effect, Whereas in other instances men and women have

been arrested directly at the gates of the
grave and given over to good health, whose
only pay rendered were ingratitude and cur-
ses. My case is not singular from other medical gentleman. But, (gracios a' Dios;) the
brightest side of this picture is to be looked
upon with examples of the greatest frequency and value to embellish it. There are no
departments of human knowledge so varied
and comprehensive; so christianizing and
philanthrophic, so true to the full benefice
of mankind; so practical and trustworthy as
the profession of medicine, including the
collateral sciences. And yet, of three great
learned Professions, it is the least in estima-
tion by the masses and by them placed as
No 3, in point of excellence and value. There
is a salient reason for this founded in the
thoughtfulness and superstition of mankind.
And I feel like digressing just enough to
give the reader the impression of one who
has reflected much upon this point. A minister is weighed by his moral demeanor
among his parishioners, as well as by his dis-
courses to his partisan people; and without
contradiction proclaims his cause and all
who hear stamps his value. His audience
can comprehend his whole field of thought;
The lawyer has a still better test; as this labor
of his life and as his oratorical talent so is

his fame to measure arms with an opposing contemporary who have an expert of their own profession as an umpire. His field is clearly one in which a true measure may be, and is always given. While the medical man has no audience; cannot advocate himself; is the subject of misconstruction; cannot measure arms with adversaries or competitors; and under some circumstances is as liable to sink and suffer for the best deeds of his life, as to soar by his merit into the arms of the "fickle god." I have given these diferences at greater length in a public discourse I had the honor to pronounce, by a regulation of the Macon Co. Med. Soc, to the citizens of Decatur, January 1868.—See Appendix.

On the 16 th day of September 1855 our third child was born. He was a fine and healthy boy, We named him Charlie, and then our little pets were the hope and splendid promise of present and prospective happiness.

Early in this year I formed a partnership with Dr. W. J. Chenoweth in the practice of medicine and continued said association for three months, when we bought out the drug house of Drs. King and Read and accepted Dr. King into the firm to be stiled "King, Chenoweth and Trowbridge." This firm continued in business for only 9 months, when I withdrew and again set out in the practice alone. The firm of K. C. & T. had sold considerable quantities of goods and did a heavy practice, giving a large book account which Drs. King & Chenoweth assumed, allowing me a cash prorata of the proffits.

My Father-in-law had moved to Decatur and lived with me since the year 1851 up to 1853 when for a short time again he removed to Chicago, but falling ill of an organic desease of the stomach, he again came to live with us in Decatur. The disease slowly but constantly increased and was the occasion of his death which took place April 21, 1855. His widow and two sons made our house their home until the eldest son Charles V. Rockwell became a graduate in medicine and located in Taylorville Illinois in 1858. Soon after Alonzo, the second son, who had learned the jewelers trade also located in Taylorville. They soon married and are now well respected and successful business men of that prosperous little city. Dr. C. V. Rockwell was a student of mine and the first who became a graduate and practitioner from my office. He married Miss Ellen Torrey, the accomplished daughter of Mrs. Torrey of Springfield Illinois. Alonzo married the youngest daughter of the Rev.

D. P. Bunn of Decatur Illinois; her beauty and accomplishments were circumscribed by no narrow bounds. She was the sweet songstress of our city, whose melodious notes brought congregations to her father's church and often fed the poor and clothed from winter's chilly blasts the needy. Her compass aud volume of voice was only equaled by its natural melody and artistic grace; and had she saught the plaudits of the stage with good support her name would long ere now have been national.

On the 15. of May of 1858 was born our second daughter and fourth child. We namod her Mattie May. Mattie was our robust and healthy babe and in all her days of infancy and childhood, gave us constant lessons in generosity and goodness of heart.

This year was one of great finantial affliction to me. I had speculated in land and town property more largely than the critical times of 1857 had justified and debts had closed in upon me to such an extent that judgements from the courts encmbered all my titles and I had to submit to some severe sacrifices in order to save myself from total failure. I was however enabled to put off the evil hour for 2 years by a series of coveyances for ready money; which, although they did not lighten the burthen yet they gave me an oportunity

of the advances in property which the two
Rail Roads and much immigration into our
part of the state was then producing. But
the political condition of the country resulting from the election of Mr. Lincoln to the
Presidency was disastrous to the embarrassed
finances of the West. I felt that I was hope-
lessly insolvent with real estate enough in
my hands to pay me out if I could but dispose of it at reasonable rates. My affairs would
not have assumed such an unfavorable shape
had I been dealt with honorably and according to those ideas of truth and justice which
regulate the dealings of honest men. Just
before the great crash of 1857 I was warned
by one of the best financiers in the state,
Mr. W. L. Powers, that the evil day was not
far distant and that it behooved me to provide
for it. I did so by an exchange of property
with an enthusiastic, loud praying, methodist
butcher; and had bargained off his property
at cash rates for a competence to clean me
from all debts. But the aforesaid butcher, al
though he often told me that "his word was
as good as his deed" and that I should go
ahead and dispose of the property the same
as though the deeds had passed until he
could get time to make them out and have
them signed yet when I presented the deeds
to him ready for his signature in exchange

for mine fully executed and signed by both
Mrs. Trowbridge and myself; he flatly refused. This transaction had occupied some 2
months during which time I had been offered a better sale for the lots I had bargained
to the butcher than he was to give me or
which I was to receive for the property I was
to get from him. He thereby prevented my re-
alizing on either until the crash came when
property ceased to sell at any price and my
provisions for the great finantial troubles
had come to no good result. The war broke
out in 1861 and I entered the army as a Surgeon and had the good fortune to pay every
cent I owed out of my monthly earnings besides giving support to my family. No one
can become bankrupt without suffering heavily in the community in which it occurs in
point of personal popularity. I was not
an exception to this rule by any means; and
only after my debts were all paid with interest was I able to appreciate to what extent
the want of confidence had gone.

On the first of September 1860 I had attended to the long list of patients and in the
evening had gone to my office to spend an
hour in reading, book posting, and office
labor and after these duties closed for the
day my work and on starting for my house
encountered a large torch light procession

of "Wide Awakes" en route for "College Hill" to hear "Dick Oglesby" speak on the political issues of the day. It was 9 o-clock P- M. and I did not join the crowd but tarried at a corner near by, to see the imposing display of torches in honor of the great "Rail splitter" Mr. Lincoln. While thus engaged my hired man came to me and said that Mrs. Trowbridge wanted me to help entertain company, and on arriving home found our third daughter, afterwards named Mary Ellen and her mother both much displeased that I was not there to introduce her ladyship to her new relations.

In 1859 I formed a partnership with Dr. George Beman, a gentleman and physician, with whom I labored with as much pleasure as was my lot with any one with whom I had ever associated. He was an able and energetic physician with an unusual amount of practical sense and whose manner at the sick room gave more comfidence and satisfaction than any man I ever saw, Our partnership cantinued until disolved that I might accept the office tendered me of Sureon of the 8. Illinois Volunteer Infantry, Commanded by Col. Richard J. Oglesby, with date of Commission April 25. 1861. We were partners something near 18 months, during which time we did a very large and widely extended practice, and received but little for it, as the war so disturbed the finances that it was mostly not collectable.

In 1860 on the 3. day of January there was issued, on my application to the Patent office a patent medical cane. This was a neat and useful invention which however has never done any body any valuable service because it was never manufactered and placed properly upon the market.

INCIDENCES OF MY LIFE AS CONNECTED WITH THE UNION FORCES ENGAGED IN SUBDUING THE GREAT REBELLION OF 1861 TO 1865.

On the call of Mr. Lincoln for 75.000 men to be furnished by the states to suppress the rebellion then initiated by the rebels in Charleston South Carolina it was allotted that Illinois should furnish six regiments. This call occurred April 17. 1861. At that time the Illinois Legislature was in session and Mr. R. J. Oglesby was State senator from the Decatur district. Immediatly upon the call he came home to Decatur and in company with Captain I. C. Pugh John P. Post and Captain J. S. Post they opened a recruiting office in the public square of our city and four days after the date of Mr. Lincoln's call for men they had two companies of an hundred men each in Camp Yates at Springfield Illinois. On the evening of the

24 th. of April a regiment was formed which had elected R. J. Oglesby as Colonel, F. L. Rhoads as Lieutenant Colonel and John P. Post for Major, with 10 companies all properly officered. Col. Oglesby promptly reported his Regiment to Governor Yates, and about two hours later Col. John Cook reported another regiment. It was arranged that the number of these regiments should commence where the Numbers of the regiments engaged in the Mexican war left off. So that the first Regiment of the rebellion was to be numbered the seventh and the second the eighth and so on. Oglesby having reported his regiment first claimed the rank and number; and Cook, coming in so closely thereafter claimed some perferment and Gov. Yates gave Oglesby the rank, and Cook the number. I feel like offering an apology for Governor Yates for making such a singular decision which can only be accounted for by knowing that he was drunk, beastly drunk. Col. Oglesby wrote to me from Springfield to come there and pass the board of Medidal examination which had been established at the urgent request of Professor J. V. Z. Blaney, Dr. Goodbrake and myself all of whom had visited Springfield self appointed to "lobby" an act of the Legislature for that purpose. I repaired before the board

and was passed and accepted as Surgeon.
Gov. Yates on the application of Col. Oglesby
appointed me Surgeon and Dr. John M.
Phipps assistant Surgeon of his regiment.
The organization of the regiment being complete it was at once ordered to Cairo Illinois
and reached there April 29. 1861. We had
no tents and but a scanty supply of blankets
and the men slept in R. R. cars and on the
ground and fared hard and rough; but offered few complaints. We were mustered into
the United States service by Captain John
Pope of the U. S. A, on the following day.

To organize a new regiment out of men
who had never handled a musket or stood in
company line is an undertaking of no small
responsibility. But the organization of the
8 th. Ill. vol. Inf, out of just such material,
was well and thoroughly effected; and her
subsequent history fully verifies this statement. We remained in Cairo drilling, block-
ading the rivers, chasing Jeff. Thompson,
organizing and executing small expeditions,
garrisoning Cairo and Birds Point until the
three months enlistment expired for which
the regiment had been organized. Meanwhile
the rebellion had assumed its full grown pro-
protions and Mr. Lincoln by the orders of
congress had called for 300.000 men and
asked that an ardent effort be put fourth to

induce as many of the "three months men" to reinlist as was possible. Every officer of of the 8 th Regt. offered their services for a three years term of inlistment and men enough was enrolled to maintain the regimental organization. Officers were furloughed to recruit and by the middle of December the muster rolls numbered about 900 men rank and file. This reorganization of our regiment was a labor of no small importance. Our experience in the past one of the expired three months was just sufficient to teach us that we had better be without men, than to take sickly and incapable ones into the service. We therefore obtained permission to reexamine and discharge any soldier or recruit whose physical organization was not up to the "regulation" standard. This order was cheerfully complied with by Col. Oglesby but met boistrous opposition at the hands of Captains. It was however punctilliously executed, and a finer display of physical perfection has seldom been seen than was presented by this closely culled regiment. I had abundant cause to feel thankfull for this rigor of selection; and Captains who at the organization of the regiments scowled frightfully at some of my rejections, in after days, thanked me with commendable frankness of heart, for saving them much trouble and giv-

ing them the chance of filling their ranks
with acceptable men. During the Fall and
Winter three small campaigns were execut-
by this regiment. One to Paducah Ky; one to
Bloomfield Mo. and one to Mayfield creek
in the rear of Columbus which latter place
was the stronghold of the rebels then on the
Mississippi river. When Col. Oglesby with
a bigade of men was on the Bloomfield campaign he was thought, by by general Grant,
to be in much danger of being met by the
greater part of the forces at Columbus then
under the Command of Lieut. General Polk.
In order to counteract a disposition on their
part to do so, an expedition of observation
was organized of the forces in Cairo and
Birds's point, to pass down on the Missouri
side of the Mississippi river and menace the
enemy at Belmont which is oposite Columbus. This resulted in a battle in which we
had something near fifty killed and two hundred wounded, I had remained in charge of
the hospital at Cairo when Col. Oglesby left
on the Bloomfield march and was therefore
on hands to volunteer my surgical services
when wanted at the battle of Belmont. Here
was my debut at the operating table of a
battle field. We were stationed at Cairo until
the 2 d. of Feuary 1862. when we received
orders to send the sick to the General Hos-

pital and put ourselves in a suitable condit-
for a long march. Then it was that I sent
my first cases to a general hospital. In breaking up our hospital at Cairo, we were leaving a field of much hard labor, a place where
very many desprate battles were fought
against desease, and where our success in
those same battles were the occasion of very
much congratulation and satisfaction. We
saw more disease and death from deseae at
this place than at any other during the war.
Here we were again examined by another
medical board appointed to inspect and examine all Surgeons of those regiments whose
period of enlistment was for three years. This
board of examination did not change my
place nor rank although it was a much more
rigid examination than the first and one
member of the board of medical examiners
was indiscrete enough to tell a friend of mine
that he wanted to become Surgeon of the
8 th. regiment; and that he hoped that, for
his benefit, I might be rejected. This member did not ask me a single question, however,
on the examination; and I had no difficulty
whatever, as the balance of the examiners
were honorable and highly accomplished
gentleman. My wife and children visited me
at Cairo and as they left for their home in
Decatur on the 2 d. of February the forces

under command of Gen. Grant took Steamer for the Tennesce river to operate against
Fort Henry. In this expedition Col. Oglesby
was given the command of the first Brigade
and placed in advance. On leaving the Steamboat I rode with him to seek a camp; in
which duty I entirely disabled a very valuable horse and was fortunate enough to obtain the use of another for a day or two of
the adjutant who was temporarily indispos-
ed and "off duty." On the 7 th. of February
Fort Henry was taken at which time Col.
Oglesby and staff were the first to enter the
fortifications from the rear. This battle was
won by the Monitors in the river, however,
and the land forces did no fighting. I was
acting as aid for Col. Oglesby and had the
good fortune to capture a rebel flag and an
excelent horse. The flag was sent to Decatur
and the horse being under age and size for
a regulation horse I was allowed to use un-
till when at Vicksburg I had him appraised
and purchased as my individual property.
He is a noble animal and has more sense,
clearly showing thought and reflection, than
any horse I ever knew. He still lives, on the
fat of the land in Illinois. We tarried 5 days
at Fort Henry and then on the 12. of Feb.
set the column in motion for Fort Donelson,
12 miles east of Fort Henry and the com-

berland river, whither the enemy had fled
and strongly fortified. Col. Oglesby's brigade
was in the advance and his abvance guard
encountered the enemy on the 13 th. about
four miles from Fort Donelson, in which
encounter several of the enemy were killed
and five of our men severely wounded. This
was the first time I was ever under fire in
an action. Here on this occasion I saw probably fifty shots nearly simultaneously fired at
two of the enemy not seventy five yards distant, who were mounted on horse-back, and
evidently surprised at our appearance at
that place, and who escaped without recieving the least injury. Two days later the hard
fought battle was won for the Union forces
over the enemy at Fort Donelson. Immediately on learning that there were wounded
men in the Brigade I left the side of Col.
Oglesny as aid and arranged depots close
in the rear of each regiment of the Brigade
and with all our hospital corps attended to
the wants of the wounded. On this occasion
the losess of the 8 th. Ill. Inf. were as follows; 56 killed dead on the field of battle
187 wounded, 13 prissners and 80 cases of
"frost bites" from the exposures in the night
after the battle. During the after noon of the
15 th. the enemy drove back our right and
surrounded two of my hospitals filled with

the wounded. But not a single surgeon left
his post, nor was a single prisoner taken
from either. I had a cabinet of over a hundred balls which I extracted from wounded
soldiers on that day; but have given them
mostly to the parties from whom they were
taken. I have a ball which entered at the
point of the left shoulder and was extracted
at the back part of the right hip, passing
superficially beneath the skin, and carrying
off a process of bone as it crossed the spine.
I have a piece of gun-barrel two inches long
and flat as a blade, taken from under the
scalp just over the left ear which evidently
had been sent there by the bursting of a
comrad's gun, which bursting was produced
by an enemy's bullet entering the said neigh-
bour's gun and doing the singular deed.
And lest I forget to mention it in its proper
place, I will now say that; at the battle of
Shiloh, I took a hideously ragged ball from
the center of the forhead, two inches deep
and which occasioned the loss of considerable
quantities of brains from both of the anterior
lobes of the brain, and the man still lives,
at last accounts, with good use of all his
faculties. Also; at the last mentioned place,
the stem of a watch with the ring and about
two inches of watch-chain, carried by a fragment of a bombshell, into the pericardiac

cavity of the heart, and this man recovered likewise. In the extraction of these articles I found the heart exposed and pulsating normally. The shell had crushed through three ribs, and in dressing the wound I found that the patient was unconscious of the fact that his heart was touched by my fingers.

I did a deed of consulting service, after the battle of Fort Donelson, for which I feel that I never had due credit rendered. Col. John A. Logan, commanding the 31. Regt. Ill. Vol. Inf., was wounded through the shoulder. It was a flesh wound; but his health, from dissipations, was such as to render him susceptible to depressing influencies, and the wound, his previous condition and the Magnesian water of Dover, gave him a very dangerous colliquative diarrhœa which was fast destroying him. His surgeon was giving him small doses of calomel and opium. Col. Oglesby called on his wounded subordinate, and with characteristic shrewdness perceived Col. Logan's critical condition, and immediately ordered me to see him. On arriving at the bedside of the gallant officer I found him unconcious, pulseless at the wrist, speechless, with a cold clamy sweat, incontinent evacuations, extensive tympanitis, and in fine all the symptoms indicating death within an hour, if a reaction could not be established very soon. Mrs. Logan having arrived at the bed-side of her husband from their home in Illinois, fully appreciated his precarious condition. After a close examination and a consultation with the attending surgeon, Dr. Million, I recommended two drachms of turpentine to be taken at once, with clysters and frictions of the same medicine. This council being at once adopted and the treatment applied, a reaction was soon established, and John A. Logan has lived to pass, with much credit and distinction, the responsible offices of Brigadier General, Major General, Congress man at large, for two sessions, from the state of Illinois, and is now, (1872,) United States Senator; and "thanks good luck and constitution" more than me for his recovery. Mrs. Logan appeared very thankful and to fully appreciate my offices in his case, and Col. L. did also, until such time as when I thought it to my interest and pleasure to decline to become his Surgeon in Chief of the Third Division of the 17. Army Corps, which he commanded. I did that in order to become Medical Director with the forces to be assigned to my old and well tried friend Maj. Gen. R. J. Oglesby, with whom I had long and pleasantly served. Althongh this was not permitted, because Gen. Oglesby

was assigned a command outside the corps
in which I was serving, and it was ordered
that I should remain with the same forces
in which I then belonged; yet, the act of
waiving my right of rank in favor of another
appeared to arouse the jealous disposition,
of Gen. Logan, and although he was never
oppressive nor expressive of dissatisfaction
or distrust, yet "actions speak louder than
words" and it was easy to see the influence
and effect of the step which had been taken
was sufficient to freeze over the warm pool
of frank friendship which had been very
easy to see before. Although I became his
Division Surgeon, and his confidence was
full and complete, yet his subsequent un-
willingness to give credit for the part I had
taken in his Fort Donelson sickness showed
his selfish jealousies. He was always mad if
Gen. Oglesby was the recipient of commendable notice; and for fear that Gov. Oglesby
should occupy some public trust which he
(Logan) might wish himself to hold, he is
now the open enemy of Governor Oglesby.
But a Major General, who, with his liberal
pay and allowances, will permit, with such
relish as to indicate almost a demand, his
staff officers to pay his mess expenses, without offering to contribute thereto himself,
can, without much consciencious disturbance,

stalk the stage of life, after having that life
prolonged by medical treatment well known
by him to be the cause of it, without returning thanks to any other source than "God
and good luck." Hence I place his coy
acknowledgement to the arrogance of a
selfish cold blooded man, who doubtlessly
feels that he has shed condescending honor
upon his medical attendant in allowing him
the privelege of treating such a distinguished
personage.

The history of the battle of Fort Donelson, as found written by Headly and others,
which I have seen, is very defective and
untruthful. Those books in particular which
take for their standard source of information
the Report of Brig. Gen. Lew Wallace;
who claims the honor of doing the hardest
fighting and of being the most important
agent in winning the victory. He was stationed on our extreme left and constituted a
part of the command of Gen. C. F. Smith, a
most thorough and impartial officer and
perfect gentleman. He did enter the rebel
fortifications first; but the enemy had drawn
off their forces principally from that part of
the battle field fronting Wallace and con-
centrated them upon our right. And, as a
good criterion to guide the doubting, I fain
would have them look carefully at the field

and then consult the records for lists of the killed and woundad, and surely he will be satisfied that the hottest of the battle was not fought in front of Gen. Wallace. There were killed on the right 929 men, and 2313 wounded; while on the left but an insignificant number, in comparison, were either killed or wounded. Gen. W's history is like his fighting, very uncertain.

The Battle Of Pittsburg Landing.

We remained a month at Dover, and then took up the line of march for the Tennessee river again where we embarked for Savanna to make a junction with the forces of Gen. Buel, then considerably to the east of us, but marching to the same objective point.

General Grant was ordered by General Hallack, whose Head Quarters were at St. Louis Missouri, to occupy a position on the west bank of the Tennessee river, and selected Pittsburg Landing as a suitable site for his forces, where he moved his army about the 15 th. of March 1862. The enemy under A. S. Johnson, desired to meet us before Buel could make his junction with Grant, and therefore attacked us at six oclock on the morning of the 6 th. of April. This was the great battle of Shiloh Church, or Pittsburg Landing; which our best generals have pronounced the hardest fought and most sanguinary battle of the rebellion.

History here misstates facts again. It says, copying after Mc Clernand's report, that Prentiss was captured early in the day of the commencement of the fight, when the truth is that he fought until after 4 P. M. of that day; and Gen. I. C. Pugh of Decatur personally talked with Prentiss not 15 minutes before the assault was made that captured Prentiss and the remnant of his command. Another thing: the Gun Boats are accredited with the honor of preserving our left wing, when Prentiss says that not a single shot from them took effect upon the enemy; but on the other hand he and his men were placed in camp, after being captured as prisoners of war, directly on the ground where the balls fell which were fired from the gun boats; and that eight of his men were wounded and killed by our own shots from those same armaments. It was daylight on the next morning before his remonstrances at such a barbarous mode of warfare were heeded, and then only at the unexpected sound of the renewal of the battle on the part of the Union forces was he relieved from the galling influences of the fire from the Lexington & Tyler.

The disgraceful disregard of Lew Wallace
to orders sent him by Gen. Grant, to move
his forces from Crump's landing and join the
combating line of battle, came near producing amost disastrous defeat, and forever
stained him with dishonor thereafter. It is
impossible to estimate the damages to national exhistance or to human life, which may
follow the disobedience of orders at such
times as those.

My part in this great tragedy was, like
all other surgeons there engaged, laborious
in the extreme.

At 6 o clock A. M. on as beautiful a
Sunday as April ever gave to admiring
mortals and while bathing and breakfast
and inspections and all the busy works of a
military camp were progressing as usual,
we heard the crash of heavy battle in front.
It was no slight brush between scattered
skirmish lines; but tremendous vollies, long
and terrific, of artillery and infantry, for
miles in extent. Soon thereafter an Aid from
Gen. Mc Clernand, then commanding the
Reserve Corps in which we were, came
galloping to the brigade Head Quarters and
gave orders for the "long roll" to be beaten
and the whole force to prepare for action
and wait for further orders. Drum Major
Fay, an old drummer from the war of 1812,

immediately stepped forth and fully appreciating the language of the dreadful din of
war in the distance, threw his very soul into the call "to arms," and never did a patriot
make that call more thrilling. The Long Roll
when properly beaten, is a singularly stirring
appeal; and Major Fay was a star drummer,
as he was a most exemplary man and noble
Christian. The reverend old gentleman, after
the completion of his summons, turned to
me, with a face beaming with sad enthusiasm
and said, "Doctor, I feel it in my very bones
that that call will give you very much hard
work to do. God grant you ample skill and
energy; and that victory may crown the
labors of the just; and may He be merciful
to those who suffer." The "Drum Corps"
of each regiment, in a battle, become assis-
tants to the hospital department; and are
used in bearing the wounded from the field
of battls to thoes places designated as field
Depot hospitals, at which places the wounded receive temporary surgical assistance. I
at once ordered Major Fay to marshal his
musicians at the Colonel's quarters, of
course subject to that oficers command, until
such time as when the regiment should become engaged, and then to deploy in search
of those who may require their assistance.
The ambulanees, instriments, medicines

Surgeons and Assistant Surgeons and every preparation for battle was immediately completed and systematically ordered to be in proper place and condition for the brigade, of which I was chief surgeon. Meanwhile the order to "fall in" could be heard in all directions, and men and officers were rapidly equipping themselves for the combat.

It was always my inclination, just before a battle, to so place myself at the head of the advancing column and, as it passed me, to observe closely every face in detail: and the language of the men of that day, as read from their countenances, was of such an impressive character that I deem it pertinent to make mention of it here There was a solemn stillness in the march, an earnestness of expression betokening a foreshadowing knowledge of coming events; which, to me, evinced the status of courage and appreciation of the surrounding circumstances with which each soldier appeared impressed. Some were pale and thoughtful, others were flushed and excited; some acted as those who would whistle down their alarm at the dark, while others with a previously rather dormant nature were arroused to a new life and vigor wholly beautiful to behold. A few were casting suspicious glances in all directions as apprehensive of present danger, and still a smaller number reported themselves suddenly sick and asked for medical assistance; but the great mass of men Went not astray. The officers appeared watchful and eager for the fray, giving short encouragements with present promises of triumph and prospective glory. They were all watchful, observant and obedient.

A colonel told me, two days before this battle, and when there was no knowledge or even a belief that a conflict was so near at hand, that he felt impressed with a feeling that an action was impending; and that he should be seriously wounded in the thigh; and asked me for a tourniquet and how to apply it in order to staunch the flow of blood. He appeared so earnest and yet so courageous that I furnished him the article with the necessary instructions as to its use; and, strange to say, his apprehensions were realized by him being shot through the thigh, in the second charge of his regiment, the ball passing through the outer portion just missing the bone, but wounding the arteria Profunda, and his tourniquet being applied stopped the loss of blood. He was promoted to a Brigadier General "for meritorsous and gallant conduct on the field of battle". I have in my recollection several similar cases coming personally to my observation, and am not aware of a single case wherein the foreshadowings were not realized   The above cited case was that of General Haynie. Colonel Dollins of the 81. Reg. Ill. Inf., predicted his wound in the head to me on the morning of the assault upon the breast-works at   Vicksburg, and asked me to give him my personal attention in case his forebodings should be realized. I promised to see him through his troubles; and in the charge he was wounded in the head, his regiment was repulsed and he was left to die on the ground the enemy had taken.   To these men the clash of the steel

> "—gave them mystical lore,
> And coming events cast their shadows before."

The men of the Reserve Corps were drawn out in column of Company; and thus arranged, awaited orders. It was but a moment before those orders came to move to the front, to support Generals Sherman and Prentiss, on whom the battle had most furiously opened. The details of this battle are now among the most brilliant events which garnish the pages of the history of our now much favored and happy country; and with the exceptions of the statements made concerning Lew Wallace and Mc. Clernand; are correct.

I went with the advancing column of our brigade until it became heavily engaged and saw that the wounded were secured from further danger and borne to the rear where I had stationed some surgeons with instructions to receive and attend to any of the wounded coming there without distinction as to what command they might belong. The first charge in which the brigade was engaged checked the enemy but did not repulse him. Meanwhile the firing on our right and left became nearer each moment and the cannon balls were falling far to the rear of the camps from which the brigade had just advanced. The wounded from Sherman's and Prentisses divisions were flocking to the rear in droves; and I soon joined the advance depot and commenced operating for the relief of the sufferers. An hour had thus passed and we had sent about six ambulance loads to the river and placed them, in good order, on hospital transports, when the firing in front ceased except as a heavy cannonade which was sending its missils close around and over us. We took this very innocently as favourable to the Union valor, but were using all our energies in getting the wonnded away in the ambulances, which were being most efficiently commanded by my very dear friend Lt. H.

N. Pearse of the Quartermasters Department. I was just then amputating the two middle fingers of a soldier who had been shot through the palm of the hand, and the operation required for its relief, was the removal of the bones in continuation of the two middle fingers at the wrist joint, leaving the fore and little fingers to make a future hand of usefullness. I was wholly absorbed in the prospect of a beautiful operation, and was just in the act of severing the bones at the wrist, when a cannon ball from the enemy crashed through the top of a large Poplar tree; under which we were at work, and felled a large portion of it immediately to the ground, precisely where the soldier had been lying and who would have been crushed to atoms had I not succeeded in heaving him out of harms way by a force much more effectual than gentle.* The

---

* My ability to rescue this man, whose weight was probably over 160 pounds, reminds me of a circumstance where a supernatural strength appeared to be given me to rescue my Nephew, F. Y. Thomas, from what I believed to be an impending death. In 1842 I was driving a two horse wagon heavily loaded and was accompanied by my little relative who fell under the fore wheel as it struck into a ditch. The weight of more than half of the wagon was resting directly across his body, and so situated that it could not be run either forwards or backwards without certainly adding to the peril. I instantly seized the hub of the wheel and only thought to make the weight as light as possible, calling at the same time to a man near by for help; but before he came I had placed the hub on my knee and then liberated one hand with which I rescued the little sufferer with but slight injury. After reaching home I tried to lift the same wheel while standing on the barn floor, and so hard did I try that I so injured myself that the effects troubled me for many years subsequent, and then failed to raise the wagon.

small limbs switched him severely, and I
broke off a thin fine blade of a bistoury in
the wound I was making. He was shot again
in the thigh slightly while in the ambulance
and escaping from this place. Thus, taking
the whole list of calamities crowding upon
this poor fellow, it could not be denied that
he was sadly abused. He was in the arena
where death and destruction were the chief
efforts of mad men; and each of his adven-
tures might have been much worse. The
falling debris of the huge tree entirely de-
molished my field chest of medicines and
somewhat injured my case of surgical instruments.

At this moment we had not more than a
dozen wounded men at this depot; I having
ordered all who could walk to seek safer
places in the rear, whither they had gone,
either by their own aid or by ambulances or
litters. Just then a driver of an ambulance
called out that "the rebs are coming not
500 yards off" and started to drive away
but Lieutenant Pearse offering to shoot at a
shorter range than 500 yards he very reluctantly halted, and we litterally cramed the
wounded into his and one other ambulance
and they made their escape. They had to
rise out of a shallow hollow and then go
some distance, a hundred yards or more,

fully exposed to the enemy before they could
gain shelter in a wood, and during this
passage six balls were put through one
of the ambulances and two through the
horses, but doing slight damage to either,
except to the man shot through the thigh,
in the case spoken of on the previous page.
All the men having thus been cared for and
conveyed to safe quarters at the river, Lt.
Pearse and I mounted our horses and
attempted to make good our escape, when
we were assailed by a tremendous volly of
musketry which did us no injury whatever,
although the enemy was less than 300 yards
distant. No sooner had we gained the brush
than we were the recipients of a visitor of
no welcome import, in the shape of a 12lb.
schrapnell shell which passed just before
Lt. Pearse and behind me, and could not
have missed either of us a foot, as it struck
a small tree just at our side, cutting it off,
and probably extinguishing the fuse; for it
did not explode. Mr. Pearse afterwards obtained the shell and sent it to his wife in
Bloomington Illinois.

We moved back to a more secure place
and there learned that the enemy had executed one of his successful flank movements on our line, and that we had adroitly
shifted ours to receive him, and hence,

these movements had occasioned the temporary lull in the firing, of which I have spoken. These movements however, had brought my hospital in the front in place of the rear, as I had intended to remain.

This thing of selecting a field hospital is not always, so easily accomplished as might appear, for several reasons. In the first place your commanding general may not feel at liberty nor inclined to expose to any one his plans of operations: then, the very ground your best judgement may select as being the most convenient and at the same time secure, for both of these elements enter into the necessities of all such cases, may be appreciated by either one or both of the contending parties, and for those very reasons, as advantage grounds for strategic movements; then again you cannot, at all times, know what disposition of the forces is transacting to disturb you from either side. You are seldom, if ever, notified of any changes which take place in your front; you are not usually furnished with field orders; you are generally intensely engaged with your surgical cases; and therefore, it is not often that you have either the time or opportunity to stand guard as it were, by giving idle inspection of the combatting columns. And so I found it, in all these

points, on this day in particular. We had
little time for meditation or in which to
operate for the relief of the wounded in this
our second location; as it was soon the very
center of another fearful collision of arms,
and hence we moved back again, and displayed the red flag of the surgeon in our
third location of this bloody field. Once more
we were soon dislodged, and then again,
and our fifth position was taken up on board
of the hospital boats in the Tennesee river.
And over these the cannon balls were flying
in numbers by no means limited. We had
been almost constantly forced back by the
enemy, and it was then 3 oclock P. M..
Already had our men stood the most furious
assaults and had given the enemy the same
for nine immortal hours without a moments
cessation. Some pieces of ground having
been taken and retaken many rimes from
each other. Our A. A. General told me that
one field sustained no less than 12 different
charges. And the havoc there manifested
would have justified the assertion had his
standard of veracity required confirmation.
At half past three the enemy ceased firing
and was engaged in concentrating for the
final charge, and spent nearly an hour in
that exercise which was, to them, a fatal
pause; for our forces in that time made

ample arrangements to receive him by planting 14 large guns in a semicircle, and abundantly manning and supporting them. Also, just at this time, Gen. Nelson, from Buel's advance, arrived on the east bank of the Tennesee river, and was immediately brought over and took position in the line of battle; giving glorious support and throwing confidence and fresh enthusiasm in our previously hard pressed and somewhat discouraged troops.

This galant act of Gen. Nelson has never received its due award of praise at the hand of the historian; because the circumstances of his days march to gain the battle ground has not, to my knowledge, been given in detail. His was the third Division of Buel's army in the line of march; and after cannons of the enemy were heard by the forces of Gen. Buel, he set his column in motion to join General Grant, he then being 18 miles distant. I think Crittenden and Mc. Cook were in the advance of Nelson as they left their encampment in the morning. They suffered some hindrance to detain them; and by the usual order of such positions and marches that delay would have stopped the whole army in the rear of the point of arrest. But Nelson, with his characteristic impetuosity permitted no obstacle to stop him; and therefore, he passed two divisions with his; and appeared ready for battle full two hours before the others came up. This act on the part of the gallant Nelson was a clear case of patriotic disobedience of orders. While discipline is the soul of success and safety in all military achievements, as a rule; yet, we are occasionally priveleged to see the salutary effects of exceptionable cases, and here was a striking one in point. This never occurs however, when selfish and cowardly motives actuate the transgressor. The eagerness to mix in the malee then so plainly to be heard; will exonerate Nelson from all such accusations. His conduct at Shiloh is quite similar to that of Admiral Nelson of the British Navy when ordered to retire from before the enemy at Copenhagen. He had given orders to advance on the enemy with his ship and when signaled to withdraw he turned his blind eye to the signal and with his glass to the same sightless organ exclaimed "I can't see it, go ahead! and was brilliantly successful in the engagement which followed. Such conduct contrasts forcibly with the disobedience enacted by the cowardly and jealous behavior of Lew Wallace who was only 8 miles distant with 8,000 men and virtually did nothing all day but to refuse assistance on technical quibbles. Gen. Grant sent two orders to Wallace – one verbal and one written in pencil – for him to move up from Crump's landing and engage the enemy, both of which orders he refused to obey in high anger, under the childish excuse that they were not proper, which he claimed should have been written with ink. His act of disobedience has rendered those pencil marks more indellible in history than he in decency may desire.

It will always be an impossibility to fully know whether Nelson was not the means by his men and the renewed confidence they diffused, of saving the Union army the great battle of Pittsburg landing. If he had remained back in the position Buell's order placed him, then, of cource, he could not have been at the battle ground at the time of the celebrated charge at half past four o'clock P. M. Nor would any of the others been there. I know that the appearance of Nelson's forces threw a thrill of joy into the flagging army of Goneral Grant; and thousands of men whose commands had been broken up and they were idly straggling on the banks of theriver, then joined the line of battle and did good service at that critical moment. Had Beauregard been successful at that time and charge, the Union army must have been overpowered and the day lost to our cause. But it was ordered different; and, in my very humble judgment, the immediate means of rescue from the perilous position, was this timely appearance of Nelson.

The enemy was repulsed after a charge lasting over one hour and thirty minutes, and each party ceased firing because of the approaching darkness, and rested each in his position on their arms, until next morning, when the battle was renewed by us with many fresh troops and great vigor. The enemy had anticipated an easy victory on this opening day, only fearing that our army might have escaped by the river transports. But, when at daybreak they were the recipients of a very destructive assault from a furious force in new and long extending lines, the rebels justly concluded that Buell had accomplished his junction. There is little doubt but that this bold dash surprised and dishertened the exultant fos more than our men were surprised and disheartened on the day previous.

This day manifested the most deafening vollies of Infantry and Artillery firing of any one in our long and bloody war, showing the death-or-victory determination which animated the contestants; but which resulted

in favor of the lasting glory of the Union
soldiery. On this day there was no drawing
back, nor technical interpretation of orders,
nor shirking from duties or flaging courage,
and the result of the harmony plainly shows
the wisdom and truth of our Nation's motto
of "United, we stand; divided, we fall."
God grant that in all coming time, that
motto or the gallant sons of those patriot
Fathers who orriginated it, may never from
necessity be baptized in another such a
stream of devoted blood as those days gave
us, in order that the Nation and Motto
may forever live in unrivaled harmony, justice and prosperity!

One more day was given to to the disorganized and badly beaten foe; and then the
sound of battle subsided to skirmishes for
53 days at which time the enemy evacuated
Corinth and sought to fortify and defend
other points of their boasted confederation.
But the labors of the surgeon did in no
manner cease with those awful days of fighting. They continued for over two weeks
before the field was cleared of the wounded.
During these two weeks we were constantly
operating. Our clothes were a gore of blood
and our hands so continuously in it that for
most of the time they were crisped and
wrinkled like a washerwoman's after a days

labor in her suds. There were in multiplied variety all the kinds of wounds on
which the surgeons skill and practice could
be exercised or was required; and he who
had an aspiration for the successful accomplishment of what is called in surgery
"major operations," had an extensive field
to make his hand familliar to the work.
The ligature of the large arteries; ampu-
tations from the shoulder joint to the fingers
and from the hip joint to the toes; resec-
tions, in which a long bone is twice divided and the injured part between the extremities removed and the extremities
brought in apposition; exsections, in which
an end of a bone leading into a joint is removed and a new end made to take the
place of the part removed; extraction of
balls, fragments shells, clothing, splinters
of wood, and various articles of foreign sub-
stances one may have about his person or
of which he may be in the close vicinity,
from various parts of the person — even the
large cavities such as the brain, lungs abdomen &c.; the adjustment and stitching of
wounded intestines; the conduct for wounds
of the brain, lungs, liver, bladder and spleen;
trephining of the skull bones; reductions of
fractures and dislocations; extraction or amputation of wounded eyes; secodary opera-

tions of all the foregoing, in consequence
of Gangrene, Erysipelas, or protrusion of
bones; treatment of anæmia or prostration
from loss or impoverishment of blood; treatment of extensive flesh wounds, burns, scalds
and frost-bites; of severe cases of shock; of
Tetanus or Lock-jaw; of exhausting supura-
tions; Gangrene, Erysipelas, the various
forms of Fevers and in fine, all the concom-
etants of injuries of whatever nature an extensive and hard faught battle gives.

In this sanguinary conflict many of my
army friends and associates were killed and
many more were severely wounded. To
them I gave all the attention possible consistant with my other duties; and be it said
to the lasting credit of those brave sufferers
that they were patient and observant of the
wants of others and fully appreciated the
multiplied duties of the surgeon. Here my
warm friend and fellow townsman Lt. Col.
Ansel Tupper was slain while gallantly
commanding his regiment in a charge on the
enemy, mourned and deeply regretted by
all who knew him and prized his intrepid
valor and glowing patriotism. Here also fell
mortally wounded, Brig. Gen. W. H. L.
Wallace, of Ottawa Illinois, commanding
C. F. Smith's Division and the center of
the army. General Wallace was a noble,

brave, discreet and dashing officer, a model gentleman, and one who enjoyed the full confidence of General Grant, which may be considered as no common preferment. He was wounded in the head, the ball taking effect in the right eye, passing backwards and outwards and lodging against the skull bones behind the ear. He received this wound at about 3 o'clock P. M. on Sunday and remained upon the battle-field until such time on Monday as when the lost ground was recaptured, when he was rescued and brought on board of the boat on which I was operating.

It had rained in deluges from about eight oclock P. M. of Sunday, and all the wounded were exposed on the battle field then in the possession of the enemy. To carry the mind of the reader to a full realization of spending a night upon an extensive and sanguinary field of battle; where saber and shell and ball and bayonet were the toys of mad mens' determinations to destroy each other, was only equaled by a thunder storm in the same night, of such terrible accents as to appear qualified to annihilate both parties, as if God were pronouncing with His thunderbolts and rain chariots an impartial excommunication and chastisement to the quarreling children of His household below, where glory and groans; courage and carnage; darkness and death were the hovering witnesses over the wounded of this horrible reality; without a cover, without a comfort, with want and woe and wounds and blood and groans and desolation such as is no where else to be found, is but a faint picture of such a condition as many felt on the dreadful night of the memorable sixth day of April 1862, on the battle field of Pittsburg Landing.

CAMPAIGN AGAINST CORINTH.

The various movements which constitute the campaign against Corinth under General Halleck, are well and correctly given by the various historians who have employed their pens in the tasks of their descriptions. General Logan, on organizing his staff, gave, as his Special Order No. 1, that I should report to his Head-quarters for duty as Brigade Surgeon, in which duty I continued until the fifth day of October 1862. Although the advance upon Corinth was called a siege, yet the place was by no means invested; and the only semblance the movement bore to such, were the works of the advancing columns upon the enemy by a

series of breastworks and concentric fortifications. The greater part of the distance
from Pittsburg Landing to Corinth was
covered by these entrenchments, either offensive or defensive, and for a breadth of
from 5 to 8 miles. From the sixth of April,
the day on which the battle of Shiloh or
Pittsburg Landing, to the evacuation of
Corinth on the 29. day of May, is called
the Siege of Corinth, and comprises 53
days exclusive of the three days of fighting
on the 6. 7. and 8. of April. Those 53 days
were arduous and exciting to the Union
soldiers because of several circumstances:
they had but so recently been so desperately
assaulted; their commands were so radically
changed and, in many insances, had been
almost broken up; the weather and roads
were extremely unfavourable; every day
gave fresh skirmishes with the enemy; reports and rumors in camp were of the most
extravagant kind; General Halleck reported
to the command in the field; troops were
constantly concentrating and we were hourly
watching for the wily foe to either flee or
fight. As we approached nearer and nearer
the lines of the enemy with ours continually
converging, the crisis was anticipated with
the keenest anxiety, the enemy meanwhile
giving battle on all promising occasions.

For all these, the Siege of Corinth resulted in the evacuation and flight from their strong position on the 29. of May, and soon our forces occupied Bethel, midway between Corinth and Jackson, Tenn., the objective point of the Reserve Corps to which I belonged.

OCCUPATION OF JACKSON TENNESSEE.

General Mc. Clernand's corps took possession of Jackson on the 12. of June, 1862, while General Grant was in command of all the forces from Cairo to Corinth, constituting the Army of the Tennessee and numbering near 100,000 men.

While we occupied these positions, many important movements and battles took place; and throughout the country many political vicissitudes were transpiring, sorely testing the vitality of our national existance. It was at this period that 300,000 more men were called for; that the Democrats were giving their strongest aid to the rebels; that the question of emancipating all the slaves was being discussed with all the bitterness of partizan strife; that Mr. Lincoln unfortunately relented in his previously wise policy of imprisoning persons in the North who were directly filling the rebel ranks, and discouraging enlistments in the union army, as well as encouraging desertions from the same; that our forces were being scattered over too much territory and their strength too much employed in protecting persons and property, instead of destroying the enemy and thereby conquering a permanent and profitable peace. It was at this period and under such rulings that the rebels would concentrate upon some unprotected outpost and capture it, taking as prisoners the defenceless garrisons to add their numbers to the prison pens at Andersonville, Belle Isle, Libby Prison and similar slaughter houses. It was by a series of such concentrations, upon such thinly scattered lines of occupation that those prison pens were filled with famishing thousands; for, in this year it was, that the fiendish barbarity was inaugurated which so deeply and indelibly blackens the quality of civilization manifested on the part of our enemies towards those whom they would fain have subjugated.

The locality of Jackson was healthy, and the season the best of the year; consequently the troops were in a splendid condition. From this position as a base, we accomplished several expeditions, contributing to the glory of the Union arms. A cavalry detachment made an excursion to Bolivar; and encountered a superior force of Artilery Cavalry and Infantry but engaged them with heavy loss to our forces, and a drawn battle, in which Lt. Col. Hogg of Bloomington was killed in a saber charge of great galantry and daring intrepidity. Col. Lawler also, with a brigade of infantry, made a similar movement against the same forces then at Brownsville, but was not successful in overtaking the enemy.

THE BATTLE OF BRITTON'S LANE.

Immediately after the expedition to Brownsville, Col. Dennis with the 20. & 30. Ill. Inf. moved against this migratory enemy, and encountered 9 regiments of Cavalry at Britton's Lane commanded by Gen. Armstrong, and ambushed in a corn field, and after being charged through and over some five times by the enemy mounted, was ultimately successful in routing him with 143 killed, and many wounded and prisoners. The Union forces suffered but little in comparison in killed and wounded notwithstanding the great disparity of their numbers, and the surprise of the foe.

This brilliant and gallant contest won a Brigadiers commission for Col. Dennis, which trust he gallantly honored to the end of the rebellion. At this place and time, my friend Doctor Goodbrake, Surgeon of the 20., and chief of the medical department of this expidition, particularly distinguished himself. He was riding by Colonel Dennis when the avalanch of cavalry assaulted the column, then not in line of battle but marching " by the right flank at will." Col. D. seeing at a glance the critscal situation, exclaimed " My God! what shall we do?" Whereupon Major Goodbrake instantly replied " fight them Colonel, by — let's have a good many of us killed before we retreat or surrender!" Col. Dennis appeared to be inspired by this patriotic appeal, and immediately threw his column into line of battle just in time to be prepared to receive the first shock of the enemy, which was a volly from carbines followed by a dash of the whole divison mounted, going through the little band of infantry unchecked. The infantry used their arms, however, with telling effect, and the designing and expectant foe was reformed on the other side to repeat the same manuel of tactics from the rear. Col. Dennis "bout faced" his line of battle, and was ready to receive his gushing visitor in gallant style. The infantry had greatly the advantage, being in the tall corn, in which position they

could see the enemy, but could not be so
easily seen by him. Men firing from on
horseback are not so effectual as the same
force would be dismounted; and our officers
were not slow in making these discoveries,
and stimulated their men by saying as much.
The battle lasted near two hours, when after
the fifth charge the enemy withdrew, leaving
the field, heavily loaded with the dead and
wounded, in our possession.

It is by no means likely that the gallant
deportment of Dr. Goodbrake will ever
find its historian to place his heroism on
record other than in these humble and ob-
scure pages. Had he, with many of his
professional associates, been fortunate to
have joined any other arm of the service
than the medical staff, such acts would have
been recognized in the official reports, and
promotions would have rewarded the truly
worthy. But as Dr. G. did not make the
proper choice of profession, the promotion,
which should have followed this meritorious
act of true courage, fell upon one more
fortunately classed, and promoted Col. D.
for whipping a greatly superion force, after
permitting himself to be surprised, and
exclaiming "My God! What shall we do?"

THE STATUS OF THE NEGRO AND THE EMANCIPATION PROCLAMATION.

This was the year (1862) which gave all the force of fierceness itself to the opposition against the policy of President Lincoln upon the question of slavery. The proclmation was a popular movement with the army, and men and officers hailed the approaching promulgation of that instrument, destined to everlasting life in letters and the purest judgement of mankind, as a harbinger portending approaching peace, founded upon principals or universal equity and justice.

There were some salient exceptions to this quite general enthusiasm, and our Brigade and Corps had frequent occasion to listen to rulings and sayings from the highest in the command which would mantle the brow of any patriot with burning blushes to hear. Some of these persons soon saw the folly of their opposition and adapted themselves to the forthcoming new conditon of things, and worked well in the new harness; not, however, without many murmurings for the love they bore for "old democracy;" while others kept up their foul calumniations in pro-slavery jargon, detraction and slander until finally, when longer forbearance ceased to be a virtue, or even admissible of further toleration, to report to their home, in semi-disgrace.

Meanwhile, the negros believed their hour of Jubilee had come, and appeared only at a loss to comprehend how many blessings it had brought, and to what extent his demands should be pushed in order that the full fruition of his new condition should be most readily obtained. He at once, on the approach of the Union army, became a wanderer from his home; usually taking whatever he could lay his hands upon, beloging to his old master, and appropriated it to his own use or amusement in his now nomadic life; and joined his fortunes with any force or party offering to accept his society. It was gratifying as well as singular to see how readily he learned the true nature of his condition, and enlisted into the better merits of a course of conduct entirely compatible with the patriotic sentiments of the union cause.

General Freemont had issued his celebrated order for the emanumission of the slaves in his military department, and Mr. Lincoln had overruled the said orders, and substituted General Halleck in command in place of Freemont at St. Louis. Gen. Halleck had promulgated, in lieu of the emanumission order, that contemptible and

impolitic "Order No. 3" which was not
an emanumission, but an insipid compromise
not meeting any feature of the contest, but
giving the fiery opposition great encourage-
ment and was the black bone of contention
and wrangle in all branches of the army

This, state of affaires was soon superceeded and rendered pacific by the Emancipation Proclamation from the pen of Mr.
Lincoln, and all parties settled into quies-
cence and took that article as the true and
conclusive law by which to be governed.
The publication of that great MAGNA CHARTA
of the rebellion put a quietus to all bickerings, and proved conclusively that the same
thing should have been done a year at least
before it was.

THE BATTLES OF IUCA, CORINTH AND HATCHIE.

The confederates after their defeats at
Pea Ridge, Fort Henry, Fort Donelson,
Island No. 10 and Shiloh, sought to re-
gain their lost prestage by concentrating
their forccs on the northern border of
Mississippi and to harrass the outposts of
the union army and even went so far as to
try the fortunes of a battle at Iuca. This
took place in the middle part of the month
of September, and resulted to the great

credit of General Grant's forces. But being unwilling to abide by the descision of one battle they renewed their tactics, and on the morning of the 5. of October 1862. appeared in front of the entrenchments they had constructed for their own defence of Corinth several months previously, and now were occupied by a Division commanded by one Davies – a cowardly villain –

General Rosecrans was commanding this and two other divisions then on the ground at Corinth. The enemy approached "in column of division" opening on the three brigades and one battery comprising the Division commanded by Davies. These brigades had been very much reduced by hard service and details so much so that the whole division did not number 3500 men, including the artillery. The right of this line was commanded by General P. A. Hackleman, the center by General R. J. Oglesby, and the left by Col. Baldwin. This division was strung out to occupy over two miles of the old rebel breastworks. It was thought by the enemy to be an easy task, therefore, to force a passage through this thin line of defense; but Generals Oglesby and Hackled man fought with a determination closely bordering desperation, and hence disputed the ground they took with so much spirit

and obstinacy that they made only about a
mile of advance in the first ten hours, altho'
their numbers were sufficient to engage the
whole line and still more to make concentra
tions and flank movements at the same time.
Col. Baldwin was wounded (?) in the thumb
and retired from the field. Davies was far
in the rear "driving up the stragglers" which
important and perilous duty wholly occupied
his high military genius thoughout the day.
leaving Generals Oglesby and Hackleman
unaided and unsupported until 3 o'clock P.
M. at which time Gen. Rosecrans came to
their relief with the two Divisions which
had up to this time been idle spectators of
the fight. Both Oglesby and Hackleman
had repeatedly sent word to Rosecrans, telling him of the situation, but he was unwilling to believe that it was anything more
than a "reconnoisance in force," and that
the division engaged was sufficient to with-
stand the enemy's feint. At 3 P. M., word
was sent to Rosecrans that the enemy had
turned our left and forced our line back one
mile, and that Hackleman was taken from
the field mortally wounded. Gen. Oglesby
was contesting every inch of ground with
the most heroic bravery until at about 4 P.
M; when he fell by a musket ball penetrating the lungs, fired by a sharpshooter not

75 yards distant. Then comes the engagement of the forces as reported by historians, involving the assaults at the forts, the penetration of the rebels to the center of the town, and finally, their repulse and radical route.

The enemy manifested at this battle a most frenzied determination and desperate bravery. The whole rebellion, probably, does not give an example of a more determined assault, nor a greater slaughter than resulted from the rashness of a Texas colonel who called for volunteers to storm the forts. He headed the movement and succeeded in capturing one, but was slain and his daring followers repulsed in a few moments after they had gained their object.

This battle was followed with a vigorous pursuit the next day resulting in an engagement on the Big Hatchie river, which was a running fight, constituting a total rout and thorough demoralization of the enemy in this part of the country.

The pursuit of this flying army brought to light the rare and valuable military qualities of General J. B. Mc Pherson, who until the time of his much lamented death in 1864, was constantly a rising man.

The two brave Generals Hackleman and Oglesby had been taken from the field in a dying condition, and placed in the principal hotel of the city of Corinth; and at 5 o'clock P. M. the rebels had penetrated to within a few yards of the same, fighting with a wickedness of will worthy to win in a more laudable cause. At this critical moment the wounded heroes were placed in ambulances and taken to the Sulphur Springs, two miles distant to the rear.

General Hackleman died soon after their arrival there; and word being sent from Rosecrans that he had gained the day, General Oglesby was returned to Corinth and placed in a private house, where his wound was examined by a consultation of surgeons and pronounced mortal.

In this consultation were Drs. Holsten, Medical Director of the Army of the Tenn., H. Wardner Surg. of Vols. and Asst. Med. Director, and several other medical gentlemen of note and ability. They had probed for the ball but could not find it.

On the next day General Grant received a telegram at his head quarters in Jackson Tenn. from Corinth stating that General Hackleman was killed and Oglesby was thought to be mortally wounded, and requested that General Grant would permit Surgeon Trowbridge to come to the assistance of Oglesby.

I was immediately ordered to report to Department Head Quarters, and was there told by General Grant what General Oglesby wanted. I at once asked for an order to go to the fulfillment of a promise I had made to General Oglesby at the time he was promoted, and left the Corps of the army in which he and I had been serving. General Grant told me he would readily give the order, but that the enemy held the railroad between Bethel and Corinth, and therefore the order would be of no avail. I said I would go by horseback from Bethel, taking a circuit around the enemy. He then told me he had no cavalry to spare as an escort, and it would not be prudent to go without one. But I was willing to take the venture, and so the order was given. This order also gave me the privelege to take as many surgeons of my Division as would volunteer to assist in the surgery necessarily to be performed at Corinth. Dr. Ormsby, Surgeon of the 45. Reg. Ill. Vol. Inf. offered to go, and at 7 P. M. we started out, fully anticipating a lively time in getting through. But on arriving, by rail at Bethel, we saw a train in the distance coming from the direction of Corinth, which proved to be Union men, greatly to the relief of our expectations, who had just then recaptured and repaired the road, giving us clear sailing for our destination " without change of cars."

On arriving at the bed-side of General Oglesby at 10 P. M., October 6., I found him pale, haggard and in much distress, incapable of lying down, with a pulse of 136 per minute, rospirations very laborious, guarded, catching and 42 per minute, expectorating small quantities of arterial and much larger amounts of venous blood, pupils of his eyes dilated, secretions much disturbed, skin bathed in a cold perspiration, excretions from the kidneys and bowels almost suspended, and compelled to sit in a semi-recumbent posture in a rocking-chair. The wound was from a musket ball entering his person at the lower and back part of the arm-pit (Axilla) on the left side, ranging directly towards the center of the lungs or asthough its exit would have been at the front and middle part of the right Axilla, had it passed through the boddy.

Gen. Oglesdy was a large portly man, weighing 225 lbs., of splendid physical developments, in the prime and vigor of life, and whose constitutional forces had never suffered from any quality of dissipations. The ball had lodged internally, and after a careful examination of symptoms (mind

you I did not probe the lungs) I concluded that the ball had passed between the
costal and pulmonary pleura, and lodged in
the body of the 4. dorsal vertebra, and that
the rough ambulance ride to which he was
subjected in going to the Spridgs, probably
disengaged it, and it fell upon the Dia-
phragm, in which position it subsequently
became enucliated. These, of course, are
but conjectures arrived at by a careful analysis of the symptoms developed from time
to time.

After my first examination was concluded
General Oglesby asked what I thought of
his chances; and I recited a well established
surgical law to him; which is, that if a person live until a full reaction of the circulation and nervous shock and is not worse
than when first shot, (it being a wound of
the lungs,) then, there are nearly always
possibilities to save life. This appeared to
encourage him for it was the first expression
he had heard since being wounded giving
any grounds for hope in the least.

To meet the indications for relief in his
case I gave him one and a half grains of
Morphine at once, to quiet the pain, to
equalize the circulation of the blood and
to give rest to the lungs by reducing the
frequency of the respirations. I very

well knew that so large a dose would further disturb the already deranged secretions and excretions, and in one hour thereafter I gave a full portion of Sulphate of Magnesia to act as an hydrogogue cathartic.

These medicines operated precisely as I had told them they most probably would. His pulse came down to 112 at 8 o'clock on the following morning, respirations 28 per minute, and he slept considerable and quite composedly during the night.

I have been thus particular in delineating the case of Gen. Oglesby and the treatment thereof, because the medical mind is considerably exorcised over the case of the late Col. James Fisk, at the time of writing these pages. The wounds were very different but the shock to the system was virtually the same. Prof. L. A. Sayer, of the College of Physicians and Surgeon of N. Y. treated Col. F. by injecting hypodermically ten grains of morphine.* Col, F. died affected with symptoms strongly indicating, to my mind, Opium poisoning. It will be remembered that the subcutaneous mode of administering morphine is a much more effective way than to give the same quantity per orum.

---

* See Report of the trial of Stokes for the murder of James Fisk,—evidence of Dr. Sayer.

At 8 o'clock next morning I met the Medical Director, Dr. J. G. F. Holsten, and exhibited to him my order from Gen. Grant to report to the care and orders of Gen. Oglesby, and told him what I had done in the previous night, inviting him at the same time to examine the patient and give me the aid of his riper judgement. He did so, and to my astonishment and consternation, recommended a plan of treatment by no means compatible with what I believed to be either indicated or safe. A consultation of surgeons had been held over General Oglesby's case before my arrival, and, he said, the course of treatment he then recommended was such as the council had decided upon in the previous day's deliberation, and he believed it to be the only course to pursue. It was to give 3 grains of opium over 3 hours, to feed him liberally on beef tea and soup and to allow him two bottles of Catawba wine per diem. I very courteously suggested the possibility of so much opium producing a specific sickness, headache and additional derangement of the secretory and excretory functions, which had already been much disturbed; saying to him that the General had taken one and a half grains of Morphine the night before, and that its action was as complete and extensive as could be desired. The doctor appeared offended at my suggestion and inquired if I had any hope of a recovery in this case? I said there were chances for hope, but of course, they were accompanied with many fears of a different result. He very bluntly questioned the soundness of a judgement of so hopeful a character, and again recounted his plan of treatment, directing me to at once go about fulfilling it. I was very much offended at both his manner and his arrogant order, and coolly and, I hope, respectfully declined to be responsible for other people's opinions; especially when they disagreed so materially with my own. I told him I had a right, according to the best voices of eminent surgeons known, to have a hope of the recovery of General Oglesby; and if I had that right and that opinion, it was my duty, in as much as I was ordered to this responsibility, to treat the case with an eye singly to gain that result. I further told him that I could not adopt his views, and begged his pardon for not accepting those of men so much my seniors in years and experience. But that I could see no chance for a recovery with opium sickness and a stomach crammed with beefsteak and the heaviest wine known to surgeons. Of course our conference broke up then, and our expressions and feelings were not such as brothers should have for each other. Dr. Holsten then went to the bed of Gen. Oglesby and began to talk to him, and I at once perceived the import of his conversation to be a recommendation for a preparation for death. I promptly called him aside and learned that such was his intention. I peremptorily forbid his doing so, and only succeeded in preventing him by assuring him that in case he did so I should prefer charges against him. He then went to Mrs. Wardner and told her that I was "an upstart" and other compliments of a like character, and asked her to send to his tent and get some opium pills, some beef and a box of Catawba wine and for her to give them to Oglesby, at such times as when I should not know of it, and in the same amount as he had recommended to me. But Mrs. Wardner was too pure and honorable a lady to make me responsible for a course of treatment I had condemned, and at once asked me what she should do? I told her to get the articles and hand them over to me; for there were 60 other badly wounded patients in the house and I had volunteered to give them full attention. And Dr. Holsten had left them in the care of "an upstart." How strange and oppressive this conduct was to me! How outrageous and unprofessional! For the Medical Director of a grand Department of the Army, and at home, a professor in the Georgetown Medical College, to so far transcend all rules of etiquette and ethics, and attempt to ride his high official position, and lord it so arrogantly over me, was the most humiliating pill the profession of Medicine and Surgery had ever presented to my humble walks while wandering in it! Oglesby took no more opium, morphine nor wine, but I allowed him a guarded diet, and even then he became jaundiced and suffered greatly from its disturbing effects; but gradually improved though slowly until the 14th of October, when I saw it was necessary to remove him from the pernicious influences with which he was surrounded. His wife, sister and brother-in-law had joined him from Decatur Ill. his home; and his staff officers remained with him; but the house in which he was lying was filled with the wounded, some horribly so, of whom I will speak more on some future page; these gave unwholsome and disgusting odors, as did the many dead men and dead horses which bestrewed the battle field. I therefore went to Jackson and reported to Gen. Grant the condition of my patient and asked for an order to remove him to his home, which was cheerfully and promptly granted. On returning I reported my intentions of removal to Dr. Holsten and requested him to appoint a Surgeon to the care of the patients I had been serving. Dr. Holsten gave the surgeon, but protested against the removal and even went so far as to get an order from the Division Commander, the coward Davies, ordering that Oglesby should not be removed. And yet at this time Holsten still said that Oglesby would surely die. On being confronted with Davies' order not to remove my patient, I drew the order from Gen. Grant from my pocket and then only were we let alone and allowed to pursue our own course with no further molestation. We made a thick mattrass of blankets on the floor of a freight car and upon this, as a cushion to break the concussions of the car, placed a rocking chair and in a semi-inclined position rode our gallant patient. We telegraphed our starting to Gen. Grant and sailed out smoothly, safely and in very good comfort. We met Gen. Grant on the platform at Jackson, who after asking if it were prudent to talk to Gen. Oglesby, congratulated him on the prospect of his recovery and at Oglesby's suggestion altered the order he had sent by me the day before, and advised his continuing his journey to Decatur. That voyage was safely accomplished and Gen. Oglesby has recovered to be twice elected Governor of the state of Illinois and is now [1873.] in the United States Senate, and holds a much better mortgage on a long and especially useful life, than Dr. Holsten. I leave the friendly reader to draw his own conclusions concerning the multiplication of anxieties and responsibilities which his meddlesome conduct occasioned. It is probably better to say now than in the chronological note, that in August, 1864 I saw Dr. Holsten at Cairo Ill. and he frankly acknowledged that he had been very wrong in his judgment concerning Ogleby's case and also that his conduct with me was extremely unprofessional and hoped that, from the frankness of his acknowledgement, I would forgive him. The victor has always the measures of mercy at his disposition; and I gave him the benefit of all the comfort the acknowledged recollection of the case would afford him.

HOSPITAL PATIENTS AT CORINTH.

I have previously said that there were about 60 badly wounded patients at the same house in Corinth in which General

Oglesby was lying. These were exclusively under my treatment during the ten days of my stay at that place. One of these was of such a remarkable character that I deem it fitting to make the history of it a part of this narrative. The subject was an Iowa soldier, an Orderly Sargent, by the name of Gage, who was shot through the body, the ball entering the abdomen square in front and passed through the bladder, the rectum and grazed the spinal column and thus escaping. The limited nature of the present treatise will not allow of a minute detail of the minutiæ of this case. But a moments reflection will satisfy any person that such a wound would be attended with great distress, disgust and danger. His condition was of the most revolting character. The hospital nurses would have as little to do with him as possible and still his condition required constant care and cleanliness and with the best of these the odors were so oppressive and overpowering that I assigned him a seperate room and gave him a very large share of my time individually. He was a splendid fellow, and all my sympathies were aroused in his favor and I had the good fortune to see some marked improvement in his case during the short time I was with him. When I left him to go home with Oglesby I gave him into the hands of the Surgeon who releived me, with a minute history of the treatment of the case, also giving the patient a letter containing the same details, which he could give to any Surgeon in the North to whatever place there he might be sent. Five months after this I had the exquisite pleasure of meeting this gentleman as Lieut. Gage, Aid de Camp on the staff of Gen. Tuttle; sound and well; and the most thankful and grateful patient I think I have ever had in all my life. He referred to the manner in which I attended him, when others shunned him and when he was loathsome even to himself to such a degree that death would have been far preferable to life, and said that next to his parents whose blood he inherited and who had guarded his infancy, he owed the next great debt of gratitude to me. It is extremely seldom that wounds of this nature ever recover so as to allow any enjoyment in life afterwards. But Lieut. Gage's case was a very favourable exception to the rule, and the fullness of his gratitude was a cogent proof of his sincerity.

During my absence in March 1862, a severe attack of rheumatism assailed my wife and reduced her very much, when Dyphtheria added its malignity to her wretched condition, and came near carrying her off. My friend, Dr. George Beman, devoted his keen discriminating talent to her case with unyielding assiduity, and succeeded in restoring her to partial health, when a violent congestive chill laid her immediately at the door of death; but that steady well balanced hand and head of skill, turned the tide of of disaster, and restored her to health.

One can only fully appreciate such services as I have had rendered by my friends Drs. Beman and Chenoweth, when it is recollected that during my employment in the army and as United States Consul, it was impossible to obtain leave of absence to go to the relief of my family myself, even if the intervening distances had not been an impassible barrier to the accomplishment of my great inclination. Our dear friend Beman died in the Fall of 1862, and his place, as my family physician in my absence, was filled by Dr. W. J. Chenoweth, who, up to the time of the writing of this paragraph, is the dearest medical friend I have left on earth.

What a galaxy of whole hearts and sound minds my medical associates have been!

Harrison and S. W. Noble, Beman, Harrison, Angel and Roberts, have all been gathered into the Good Shepherd's fold, while King, Chenoweth, Rockwell, Lewis, Allison, and in the army, Goodbrake, Kitto, Perley, Ormsby, Denison, Hill and Brundage—sound men in head, hand and heart—nor should the list stop here by an hundred names or more, but these are those whose copartnership or association made our walks more close and intimate in times and tests which tried the magnitude of men.

AT JACKSON TENNESEE.

While we were lying at this place, the Surgeon-in-chief of the Reserve Corps, Dr. Perley, was promoted to the office of Medical Inspector General of the U. S. Army and stationed at Washington D. C.. Soon after his accession to that office, he wrote to me, then at Jackson, asking me to become one of his Medical Inspectors. A law had just past Congress, creating eight more Medical Inspectors, and he, the chief of this Department, wanted me to serve as one. It was a promotion which I very much desired, and I at once informed him that an appointment would be acceptable. The appointment was to be made from surgeons of the Regular Army and from Surgeons of Volunteers. I was neither; was only a regimental surgeon. It was necessary for me,

therefore, to pass a board of medical examiners, and receive the appointment of Surgeon of Volunteers in order to be available
for this position. Consequently I applied
for examiation and, was cited to appear
before the examiners in Washington, Dec.
29. 1862. The date of the order citing me
to this examination was October 13. 1862.
I staid in Decatur with General Oglesby
until Dec. 26. and then left him to meet
the medical board in Washington. On arriving there I called on Colonel Perley and
told him I was fully "crammed" for the examination, and anxious to meet the men who
were to test my caliber. He introduced me
to the Surgeon General who told me that
on the 18. of Nov. he had issued an order
prohibiting any more examinations for Surgeons of Volunteers, and that I must be examined for an assistant surgeon of volunteers
and when a vacancy occurred for a surgeon
of volunteers, that it would be filled by promotion from the grade of assistant surgenns.
I told him I had encountered considerable
expense, and traveled a long distance on
the order citing me to appear for examination as a surgeon of Volunteers, which
order had never been, to me, either counter-
manded or superceeded; and that I was
ready for the examination; but that I did

not want to be promoted downwards. I was already a surgeon having passed two boards of examination and seen much hard service as such. That had his order of Nov. 18. been sent to me I should not have pursued the bubble any further. I also stated that my whereabouts had been regularly reported giving no excuse why I had not been notified of the order prohibiting examinations direct for surgeons from any rank of merit.

The Surgeon General saw the situation clearly, but would only promise that "if I passed the board with a first class grade of merit he would promote me to the first vacancy presenting." I frankly told him that such a course would be a greater injustice to those who were then assistant surgeons of the first grade than to allow the board to examine me on his previous order of Oct. 13..

The Surgeon General was Hammond, whose trickery and traffic in his official position secured the well merited disgrace which a military court-marshal meeted out to him, by cashiering him for high crimes and misdemeanors.

This, therefore, was a signal failure; and I returned to Decatur, without an examination. I found Gen. Oglesby able to take care of himself, and asked for an order to

report to my regiment, then at **Memphis,**
Tennessee, which was given, and on about
the 20. of January 1863, I joined my old
comrades at that place. It was there and
time that I waived my right of rank in favor
of my friend Dr. C. Goodbreak to hold the
office of Surgeon in Chief of the 3. Division
of the 17. Army Corps, then commanded by
Gen. Logan, the consequences of which are
given on pages 58, to 61. I therefore remained with my regiment—the 8. Ill. Vol.
Inf.–until we passed down to Lake Providence, Milikens Bend and Youngs Point,
which is just opposite Vicksburg. At Lake
Providence Gen. Grant made the attempt to
utilize Bayou Tensas, which leads from the
lake to below and back of Vicksburg on the
west side of the Mississippi, by cutting the
levee, and thus letting the high water of the
Mississippi into the bayou, thereby hoping to
be able to run boats from the river at Lake
Providence through Bayou Tensas into the
Mississippi below Vicksburg. But this and
his canal at Youngs Point were failures. It
then became necessary for a bolder push of
strategy to be made, and Gen. Grant prepared six steamers to run the rebel block-
ade at Vicksburg. On the 18. of April 1863,
two or three iron clad gunboats passed the
batteries in the night, and cleared the river of

all warlike crafts for a long distance below Vicksburg. On the night of the 22. of April the six transport steamers with about twenty men on each, who had volunteered for the work, started on the perillous enterprise of passing the rebel batteries. The first boat commanded by Lt. Col. Oliver of the 7th Missouri Inf. was sunk: but the crew escaped; and all the others went past the batteries all more or less disabled. The one called the "Old Continental," and on which those of the 8. Ill. Inf. volunteered to go, received 43 cannon balls through her, one of which plunged through her machinery cutting the steam-pipe and totally disabling her movements. Another shot struck her on her water line which was corked, by the gallant crew, with a bale of cotton. Lieut. Mc.Clunn was standing on the hurricane deck, when a shot struck the bell by his side knocking it into fragments, and him into the water. He swam to the barge in towe and regained his position, with no other injury than a very cold bath just at a time when he did not think he needed one. The same shot mortally wounded private Mc.Carty, acting pilot. I was invited to witness this gallant feat of courage, by going on board of Gen. Grant's steamboat, the "Henry Von Peul" which followed the fleet until cannon balls passed freely to a long distance to our rear, although none struck the boat. The enemy had set houses on fire along the banks of the river to give them light, and opened all their batteries on the fleet with tremendous effect. I never had heard heavier cannonading than was visited upon those devoted patriots who manned these boats; and for five miles they poured their destructive missils into these defenseless voyagers; some of them only going with the current which carried them within a few rods of the shore nearest the enemy. The successful passage of these five boats made, with the three gunboats before mentioned, gave Grant a sufficient fleet of transports and convoyes to effect a crossing of his army to the east bank of the Mississippi river. His army was accordingly set in motion from Youngs Point, Milikens Bend and other points in contiguity at which troops were stationed, marching on the west bank of the river until they reached Hard Times landing, which is about 35 miles below Vicksburg. Here Dr. Goodbreak fell dangerously ill and requested Logan to relieve him of his command as Surgeon in Chief of his Division. He did so, at the same time sending for me to report to his Head Quarters, for the duties of that office. I did so cheerfully, well knowing that we were on the eve of decisive movements of no ordinary character. The surgical arrangements had been thoroughly organized for the whole army, and the various Operating Boards appointed for each Division. I had been appointed Director, or Chief of the Board of the Third Division, and when Surgeon Goodbrake fell sick, his duties devolved upon me in addition. I had, however, the following named surgeons in my command, whose urbanity and ability were of the most consoling support, the recollection of which and whom, gives me the warmest emotions of gratitude. Dr. Angel, of the 124. Ills. Dr. Harrison, of the 68. Ohio, Dr. Hill, of the 20. Ohio, Dr. Brundage, of the 32. Ohio, Dr. Reeves, of the 86. Ohio, and Dr. C. N. Denison, Asst. Surg. in charge of the 8. Ills.

With these men there were no bickerings nor jealousies, but all were able, energetic and harmonious. Each regiment had a Surgeon or an Asst. Surgeon to attend to the wounded as they fell on the field of battle, who applied such dressings as were immediately necessary to save life, and to spare pain, until they could reach the operating board of the division, where were four surgeons fully equipped with all necessary implements to attend to the complete disposi-

tion of all cases requiring operations. The
organization of the medical corps, as effected at Hard Times landing, was continued
until long after the capitulation of Vicksburg. and was as follows viz.

S. T. Trowbridge, Surgeon-in-Chief of
the Division, and Chief of the Board
of Operations;

Surg. Angel, Superintendant of hospitals;

Surg. Reeves, Register of Board of Operations;

Surgeons { Harrison, }   Board
              { Brundage, }   of
              { Hill, }   Operations.

A hospital was established at Hard Times
landing; and 60 very bad cases of various
diseases left there, among whom were my
friends Surgeon Goodbrake and Captain
Lloyd Wheaton. I detailed an Assistant
Surgeon from the 124. Ill. Inf., an elderly
man, to take charge of this hospital, leaving
medicines and provisions sufficient for their
use, and with the army crossed the river to
the state of Mississippi, on the first day of
May 1863.

BATTLE OF MAGNOLIA CHURCH.

On the evening of the 30. of April, the 13th Army Corps crossed the Mississippi river at Hard Times landing, and on the morning of the next day, the 17th Corps joined them, and immediately marched to meet the enemy then about 12 miles distant at Magnolia Church or Thompson's Hill, four miles S. W. from Port Gibson, Miss. Here the enemy made a determined stand, although in very inferior numbers to the Union forces. The battle lasted from 10 o'clock A. M. until dark, principally sustained by the 13th corps, although heavy skirmishing was done during all this time by the 17th corps. General Grant could not know the relative force absolutely that was pitted against him; nor was he certain that the principal part of the enemy under Pemberton had not marched from Vicksburg to meet him. Grant had so recently crossed the river that scouts and spies had had no time to obtain reliable data, and he had consumed eight days in moving his army from Young's Point and Milliken's Bend to the point of crossing the river at Hard Times landing. Although this distance was but 35 miles direct, yet the shape of the country and overflowed lands, rendered a march of over 100 miles necessary: then, his artillery, ammunition and supplies, were unavoidably so heavy that it was a master feat of energy to accomplish the march in even so short a time. These circumstances could not well escape the attention of the vigilant enemy, and hence the prudence and caution of this day at Magnolia Church was but another manifestation of that stern sagacity which has characterized the movements of General Grant.

We only had about 50 men wounded on this battle field, which was less than half a patient each for the surgons there to relieve them. But the enemy was not so fortunate. They had many more wounded, and their surgeons were of the most ordinary kind, of whom we captured six, giving them medicines, instruments and all the attention required to provide for their wounded.

At this battle field I had an opportunity of observing a specimen of surgery performed by the captured rebel surgeons, which was more certainly destructive to the confederate cause than Yankee bullets. It was this: a rebel soldier had been wounded by a buck shot or pistol ball penetrating the thigh bone about two inches above the knee joint, from directly in front. The wound was very simple and did not fracture the bone. They decided to amputate the thigh and placed the patient on the table; and their decision being overheard by some of my surgeons hastend to me and told me of the case and their determination. I immediately repaired to the table, at which they were operating, examined the wound carefully, and told them it was a case which did not justify amputation. They said the thigh bone was split, and the ball still in the bone; and still insisted on the operation. We argued for a trial to save the limb, saying that subsequently, if it became necessary they could remove the thigh. But they intimated that they, as surgeons, would not be held as prisoners of war, and that the only chance for them to operate would be then. We told them that their comrade would be cared for with ability and full humanity by our surgeons, if they, or some of them, were not retained to take charge of their own wounded. We also told the wounded man that, if he objected to the amputation, we would not permit it to be performed. We then left them for other urgent duties; and returned in about half an hour, when they were just in the act of amputation. They had applied the Spiral Tourniquet high on the thigh, to arrest the hemorrhage; and were operating by the flap method. The operator had transfixed the thigh with his Catline so closely to the tourniquet band that the blade came out above it on the inner side of the thigh. He made his sweep forming the under and inner flap first, cutting, of course, the tourniquet strap in doing so, and severing the Femoral Artery at the same time. They attempted to compress the artery in the groin, but were so much excited that the loss of blood caused the death of the poor deluded soldier in a very few moments after the thigh was removed, and before the dressings had been applied or he taken from the operating table. Dissection proved that the bone had not been split, and that the amputation was perfectly unjustifiable. So much for rebel surgery. Their armies suffered terribly for want of competent skill in this department, although there were many highly accomplished surgeons in the Southern forces. But the great majority of those with whom the collision of arms brought me in contact, were of a very inferior grade.

Next day the enemy retreated, crossing and burning the bridge at Port Gibson, which our forces reconstructed and passed with but little delay. Our march to Willow Springs gave no incidents worthy of note;

but here a report reached us that the hospital I had left at Hard Times landing was in a horrible condition: that the men were dying for want of food, medicines and medcal attendance; that Dr. Goodbrake and Captain Wheaton were not expected to live two hours; and that the doctor in charge was drunk. General Logan wanted me to give an explnation of how this could be; and I promptly predicted the falsity of the report, but asked to recieve an order to cut across the country and visit the hospital. General Logan was anxious to comply, in as much as the army was to remain at Willow Springs from 36 to 48 hours, waiting for General Sherman's corps, the 15 th, to come up. He (Logan) went with me to General Mc. Pherson, who said the road to Hard Times landing was beset with straggling scouts of the enemy, and that he could spare no escort. I told him I would go without an escort, and be back before the army moved from its present camping ground, should he tarry his appointed time, and he added "and, if you are not captured." Gen. Mc. Pherson gave me the order, and I with my orderly, started for Hard Times landing, a distance of 30 miles, at 8 o'clock P. M., May 9th 1863. It was a moonlight night with straggling clouds, and the roads were good, extending over a rolling country. My orderly and I had made about half the distance, when on a sudden there was a broad and vivid flash instantly followed by a tremendous and almost deafening explosion with a continuance of the flashing, but the detonations were more endurable. I caught the direction of the scintillations, and at once recognized the phenomenon to be the explosion of a monster meteor. My orderly was a very superstitious young Swede, and although bold and intrepid in battle, was now filled with terror of the most overwhelming kind at beholding this grand and most magnificently beautiful exhibition of nature. Nor could I pacify his fears until I told him that it betokened our success and prosperity. I thought that, if he must have a whim concerning the beautiful visitor, I would give him a comfortable one, as best suited to his extravagant fear. It was truly a frightful explosion, very similar to a salvo of heavy artillery, and almost made my hair to stand erect, for I expected to see the foe bristling around us and demanding an unconditional surrender. The reader will hardly be able to fully appreciate the double joy I felt when I beheld this salute from the windows of heaven in lieu of being tethered in those death-dispersing prison pens of Andersonville, Bellisle or Libby prison, as an ultimatum.

We reached the Mississippi river opposite Hard Times landing at day-break, and found the place garrisoned by a small guard with pickets posted for a mile or more on the road we traveled. We had little difficulty in passing these pickets, and found General Sherman with his corps just beginning to cross the river.

On reaching the ill reported hospital, I found it in a most prosperous condition — all recovering finely; not a death having occurred; with plenty of medical supplies; all neat and clean; and every one well satisfied with the able and attentive treatment of the entirely sober and temperrte surgeon I had left in charge. My task was therefore, a pleasant and short one to perform, and we, that day, again rejoined the army at Willow Spings, without further incident worthy of mention.

BATTLE OF RAYMOND.

General Sherman crossed the Mississippi river with the 15th Army Corps and joined General Grant at Willow Springs. The enemy had sent out from Vicksburg all his available force to contest all favourable points, and such an one presented itself about 4 miles S. W. of Raymond Miss., at which place the advance corps under the command of General Mc. Pherson, reached, on the morning of the 12th of May, 1863. This battle was a severely and stubbornly contested one, especially on the part of the rebels.

The three Army Corps of Gen. Grant, constituting the Grand Army of the Tennessee, the 13th, 15th and 17th, commanded respectively by Mc. Clernand, Sherman and Mc. Pherson; were respectively composed of 3 Divisions, each division of 3 Brigades and each brigade of three or more Regiments. Some of the regiments were very much reduced in numbers, and when such was the case, the brigade took more regiments to raise the troop to about 1,600 men, or a division to about 5,000; and with artillery and cavalry, to near 6,500 men. It will be seen therefore, that General Grant had nearly 60,000 men well equipped and thoroughly drilled. Hence the "lost cause" must needs offer his most determined resistance.

This army was to press forward upon the enemy by 3 parolel roads, the right being given to Mc. Pherson, the left to Mc, Clernand and the center to Sherman. Our objective point was of course, Vicksburg; but we were more than 40 miles to the S. E. of that place, and the enemy over 40,000 strong to the N. E. and N. of us; active, vigilant and keen to fight whenever an advantage presented. Besides these 40,000, which constituted Pemberton's command, or the Vicksburg army, Gen. J. E. Johnson was marching to the relief of Pemberton from an easterly direction, and had ordered Pemberton to engage us from the Vicksburg front, at as early an hour as was possible, while he (Johnson) would come by the way of Jackson and Raymond, to the field of battle whenever that should be.

The sound of musketry and artillery in front of Mc. Clernand, showed the position held by the enemy: this was but a short duel of skirmishing; and soon thereafter the same kind of music was heard in front of Sherman. This also was of short duration, and then the next heard from the foe was

a volly at Mc. Pherson's advance, disputing the passage of a small bayou, fronting
General Logan's Division. This stream was
skirted by a thick wood, and served as a
breastwork for the confederates. Logan's
division was soon hotly engaged in a general
battle, and for three hours the missels of
war were exchanged with a fierceness and
spirit, on both sides which plainly showed
the estimated importance of the stakes
played for, to be of no small consideration.
Logan had ultimately pressed his left close
upon the enemy's right, and then ordered
that wing of his division to charge across a
narrow level corn field, and thus to turn and
destroy the enemy's line in that part. This
order fell upon the first brigade commanded
by Brig. Gen. M. D. Legget, with the 20.
Ill, Infantry on the extreme left. Upon that
gallant though small regiment, the main resistance of the foe was directed, and succeeded in stopping our advance, but did not repulse us — the men lying closely upon the
ground, partly shielded by the furrows in
which the young corn was growing. Gen.
Mc. Pherson seeing this state of affairs,
ordered Logan to reinforce his left from
his right brigade. Logan, with his Staff,
dashed across the field, from the left to the
right, under a galling fire, and ordered

the 8th Illinois Infantry to rescue the 20th. This was all done upon an open field, with but a very few rods intervening between the two contending columns. On arriving in "double quick" time where the 20th was lying, the 8th charged, still at double quick, upon the enemy, and delivering a deliberate and deadly volly into him at not over 5 rods distance, then charged with the bayonet, when after a short clash of these weapons, routed him and thus, gloriously gained the day.

This was the only bayonet charge I witnessed during the rebellion. That dash of General Logan across the field was one of those gallant acts which would be best described by an artist capable of drawing a dashing officer at full speed, flying just at the rear of a fighting line of battle, upon a white charger, in full uniform, with his hat in one hand, his sword in the other and both brandishing in the air, ejaculating commands and encouragements to the men as he passed them, in terms and expressions as only John A. Logan could give them, or more forcible than his present ideas of the Methodist Discipline would justify. Two orderlies of his staff were wounded, in this movement, but he and his officers escaped unharmed.

General Mc. Pherson immediately occupied Raymond, and forces were sent in pursuit of the flying foe. We had many wounded and slain, and the succeeding 24 hours were employed, by the surgeons in disposing of the unfortunate; but so thoroughly systematized was our work that, at the end of that time, the job was accomplished, and the wounded placed in hospitals at Raymond with surgeons, attendants, medicines, instruments and supplies left to follow up those cases upon whom operations had been performod.

In this battle fell the gallant young Maj. A. Leeper, of the 8th Ills. Vol. Inf. who had that day been promoted to that office; also Lieutenant Colonel Richards of the 20th, both dying within a few hours after receiving their wounds.

The following extract is from a report I made to the Medical Director, immediately after the fight, concerning the incidents of this battle, and pertaining to the interests of the Medical Staff.

"The nature of the wounds recieved, and the constitutional shock to the system was very grave and severe, and it was observed that there were scarcely any balls to be extracted; but that they had passed through the persons. It was also observed that bones through which balls had passed were very much comminuted, and when crossing any of the long bones, rendered their removal, either by amputation, exsection or resection necessary. It will be seen by a perusal of the 'Tabulated Statement' (which is herefrom omitted) that our men were wounded in all parts of their persons, as would naturally occur when the whole man was exposed to the enemy's view and fire.

The wounded men appeared much depressed and shocked, and reaction from injuries not satisfactory. The previous health of this Division had been, and is still, most excellent: yet, the mortality, from the foregoing causes, is unavoidably large. The surgical care and treatment were timely and able, the medical supplies and hospital stores were sufficient, the site of the hospital was handy and healthy, the stewards, nurses and cooks served with system, energy and cheerful care; and the ambulance system introduced by Medical Director Mills, operated, on this occasion, with most excellent effect. A foraging party was dispatched early for all supplies which the country furnished or the wounded required, which soon returned with a full supply of needed articles both of food and cooking utensils."

BATTLE OF JACKSON, MISSISSIPPI.

On the day following the battle of Raymond, General Grant set his forces in motion for Jackson Mississippi, leaving a division at Raymond, and another near the railroad at Bolton. We camped that night between Clinton and Jackson, and early next morning broke camp for Jackson, in a terrific rain storm. General M. M. Crocker, commanding Quinby's Division (the 2nd of the 17th corps) was in the advance, and encountered the enemy occupying a ridge commanding an open field sloping to a ravine, difficult to pass with artillery, at which, Crocker was very furiously engaged, when Logan came to his support. From this ravine to the ridge was about 400 yards, and over this ground was a fierce artillery duel passing between the combattants. General Crocker ordered a charge by the infantry, which was the prettiest display of military maneuvers I ever beheld. They marched in line of battle, slow and steady, as though they were on parade with an immaginary foe in front, all the time recieving a deadly and destructive fire from the enemy on the ridge, who were concealed by a hedge in part and by a wood for the

remainder of his line. Our forces were all
in the open field, and the movement plainly
to be seen by a spectator located as were
the Staff of General Logan. This firm,
measured and resolute charge of General
Crocker's Division called from that Staff
of officers including General Logan, no
stinted commentaries of praise. The issue
was soon at hand, for the "secesh," after
recieving a deliberate volly, saw that the next
compliment to be bestowed, was the bayonet;
and their experience, at Raymond, in "cold
steel" was not a pleasant nor profitable
recollection, and they broke in confusion with
a yell almost equaling their vollies and the
thunders from the clouds then peeling.
They charged them so hotly that when they
gained the sally-ports of their breastworks,
which were only some 350 yards behind
where they had made their stand, they
could not reorganize for the defense of those
works, but fled beyond and whereve precipitate flight offered safety. They set fire to
some Caissons filled with "fixed ammunition" packed in cotton, as they passed
through their fortifications where these
caissons and cannons were stationed. Major
C. S. Stallbrand, Chief of Artillery on
Logan's Staff; had obtained permission for
himself and me, to pass to the right flank of

the fighting column, to inspect and watch that part of the engagement. We arrived there just as the enemy "skeddaddled," as it was very expressively denominated in those days, and Stallbrand, seeing the rout to be complete, called out "let us be the first inside the rebel rifle-pits," and dashed off at full speed, followed very closely by myself. We, being mounted, outran the infantry, and entered close at the heels of the "rebs."

Major Stallbrand seeing the caissons on fire, ran to them and grabed the blazing cotton in time to save the explosion of the ammunition and the burning of the carriages.

I could not help censuring him for his rashness in doing such an extremely dangerous act, when no human life was to be saved by it. But he said he knew they had no time to cut the fuses of any of the shot, and did not think much of the peril or danger. He was a thoroughly educated Swedish officer and knew no such feelings as fear. His cool reflection and philosophy concerning the actions of the flying enemy, at that exciting time was so complete and correct that to him he felt no fear of accident because of his comprehensive knowlege of this department of warfare.

My Division not being engage at this battle we had no wounded to attend to and I therefore, offered the services of the whole division to Dr. Twitchel, Surgeon in Chief of Crocker's Division. He thankfully accepted my courtesy, and we made short work of a big job, or what to them would have been such. Meanwhile Logan's Division changed position and when night came, those of us who had remained to see the last man comfortable, sought our commands, being told that Logan had camped in the woods to the south of Jackson whither we went in search of him, but became misdirected and straggled to a distance of two miles or more on the road the enemy had taken. We here met Dr. Huitt, the Medical Director of the army, who was in search also, of General Grant's Head Quarters, which, he said, was with General Logan. Dr. H. insisted that we had not gone far enough to find them, and we all went still farther until we came to the railroad; and there we saw a train of cars approaching us. I told our companions that that train could hardly be in the hands of Union soldiers and coming from that road and direction. Dr. Huitt scoffed at the idea and said he was going to see; and did so. We returned; and he passed eight months in Libby Prison for his judgement; narrowly escaping starvation and death from Scurvy in that charnal house.

We spent the night at the house of the Rev. Mr. Hunter in the suburbs of Jackson and relieved many fears that reverend gentleman had conjured up concerning the ferocity of the Yankee Soldiery.

BATTLE OF CHAMPIONS HILL OR EDWARD'S STATION.

General Grant now having gained three decisive victories over the enemy, and fully appreciating the condition of the divided forces in his front and rear, determined to "move immediately upon his works" again, and thence set out from Jackson on the 15th of May, with all his army, to intercept, if possible, the junction of the rebel forces in Vicksburg. He therefore ordered Sherman to guard Jackson with a part of his corps, and dispatched orders to the division at Raymond commanded by General Mc. Arther and another near there commanded by F. P. Blair, to push forward to Edwards Station with all possible dispatch. This station is situated some 11 miles on the R. R. from Jackson towards Vicksburg. Gen. Mc. Clernand was ordered to support this column by General P. J. Osterhaus' division. Osterhaus was a gallant and prompt officer, and had the order been delivered to him it would have been obeyed at once, as he, Mc.Arthur and Blair had but a few miles to go to accomplish this march, while those from Jackson had thrice their distance to march; and at the same time were the men who had done the fighting of the three previous battles; and yet, they were on the battle ground, May 16th, and three hours engaged, before Mc. Clernand could be heard from.

General A. P. Hovey's Division was in the advance and encountered the foe deployed upon a hill and sloping ridge of slight elevation, which were covered with heavy timber and a thick under-growth, bounded by open fields descending to a broad level alluvial plain on our right.

General Logan's Division occupied a position on the extreme right and almost at right angles with Hovey's Division and were in the open filed, but covered by a hollow. He pushed Robinson's battery to the brow of the hill on the left flank of the enemy and but an hundred yards distant from their lines while Degolia's Battery was stationed about 400 yards to the rear and a very little to the right of Robinson and on the opposite hill to which the latter was placed. Robinshn's Battery was double shotted with canister and Degolia's with shrapnell. The infanty of Logans division was just at the rear of Robinson's battery and of course in front of Dagolia's. Thus they waited ready to swing round to the right and meet Mc. Clernand, thereby surrounding the enemy. Hovey becoming very heavily engaged was gallantly supported by Crocker and then they rushed the foe backwards, recapturing the lost ground. Robinson advanced and uncovered two guns of his battery, opening upon the "rebs" not 100 yards distant. This was a feint, and took splendidly. For immediately we could see the confederate officers rallying their men for a charge upon this fraction of a battery. Soon they came with bayonets fixed at "trail arms" and double quick. Immediately Robinson placed his other 4 guns in line with the 2 advanced ones and opened with all six peices double shotted with canister as I said before. At the same instant Degolia opened with 6 guns and shrapnell and the infantry advanced to a line with Robinson's battery, and gave them a raking volly, when the "rebs," seeing they were in dangerous ways, retraced their steps with a "puick" faster than is described, as a gracefull movement, in any work on military movements I ever read.

At this time Mc. Clernand could be heard thundering on our extreme left, but rather to Logan's right, as he was in the rear, for Grant's movements were so shaped that his lines formed nearly a circle, when Logan charged heavily to the right, and capturing 1,600 prisoners. This closed the fighting for the day although General Oster-haus was ordered to pursue and if possible prevent the enemy from crossing Big Black River on the R. R. and wagon bridge. This he gallanty attempted, but failed in the main part, but captured many peices of Artillery and a train of stores and ammunition, when night coming on he was compelled to desist, sleeping on his arms in a very advantageous postion for offensive movements on the next day.

I sat upon my horse by Degolia's battery at the time of the ultimate charge, which is before decribed, and seeing its terrible effect, proposed to Dr. Brundage and Captain Whitlock to immediatly visit the place where the enemy had so recently been, and where we expected to see hundreds killed and wounded. Although the smoke had scarcely cleared away before we were upon the ground, and we therefore saw all that was there, yet we found but three dead and 10 wounded. The God of Battles must have spread His mantle of protecting charity over those erring mortals there exposed; for surely, it appeared absolutely impossible that a single soldier could have escaped such a raking infilade as that was with his life! As the fleeing foe were attempting to escape up a precipitous bluff, they became fully exposed to Logan's infantry, and there the slaughter was terrible.

Our surgical experience was principally for our captured wounded enemy, and I had selected an aisle of negro quarters for my Division Hospital, and collected a company of "stragglers" for the hospital guard by permission and approval of General Grant. In the morning at just day-break, my Chief of Ambulances dashed at this hospital guard and thoroughly stampeded them, so that I saw no more of them thereafter. Our surgeons worked all night to complete their duties, and early next morning we left the wounded well supplied in every want for their comfort and recover. But all those were taken from this hospital afterwards by some straggling "gorillas," leaving those poor fellows suffering terribly for the want of every thing which wounded and sick soldiers may be in need. During the night we performed many of the major operations of surgery by the light of but one candle, and that of the most inferior quality. I rode three times over the battle field that night attended with an ambulance to be certain that all the wounded should be cared for, well knowing that we would be ordered forward early next morning; which was the case.

BATTLE AT BIG BLACK RIVER.

The failure of Mc. Clernand to comply with the order to occupy Edward's Station, permitted the enemy to retreat with most of his forces and munitions of war towards Vicksburg. Sherman was ordered to occupy Bridgeport, now upon our right, and early on the next morning, May 17th, the whole army was in motion and offensively advancing upon the disconcerted enemy. General Osterhaus charged him, at day-break, with such consummate tact and energy, from the east bank of Black River—a low marshey stretch of wooded river bottom—and most admirably succeeded in capturing over 4000 prisoners and 17 pieces of artillery, with but slight loss to himself. At the commencement of this battle the confederates occupied both sides of Black River; the west bank was a precipitous bluff extending to the river's edge, and when those on that bank saw their comrades defeated, they sat fire to the bridge to prevent the passing over of the Union army, thereby cutting off all chances of escape for their own forces on the east side of the river as well. Hence the easy capture of provisions and cannon.

Sherman had reached Bridgeport, and having with his forces all the pontoons in the army, crossed over, and early on the morning of the 18th of May was on his way to the right flank of Vicksburg.

During the night of the 17th of May, General Grant's forces had constructed a floating bridge at the site of Osterhaus' victory on Black River, just above the burnt one, and by 8 o'clock A. M. his army was crossing; Mc. Clernand taking to the left by the Baldwin's Ferry road, while Mc. Pherson, in the center, marched direct for Vicksburg by the Jackson road.

Before the sun had set on the 19th of May General Grant had completed the investment of Vicksburg, surrounding a foe of near 40.000 soldiers, and now besieged him in the strongest fortifications of the boasted confederacy—" the Gibralter of the Mississippi" with an army of about 60 000 men.

When a careful study is made of the correct history of this campaign up to this time, the impartial critic must confess that the erudition, judgement, schemes and ex-

ecutive skill which effected it, have rendered
it noteworthy and remarkable when measured by the most successful ones of any
nation at any time since the world began.
Nor does the subsequent scene in the grand
tragedy subtract one jot or tittle from its
glory; but adds imperishable laurels for the
brilliant achievements of the Grand Army
of the Tennessee.

THE SIEGE OF VICKSBURG.

The siege of Vicksburg was the crowning glory of all those military events with
which my humble services were connected.
Although General Grant's forces rested
upon the Mississippi River above and below Vicksburg, and General Mc. Pherson's
Corps joined both Mc. Clernand and Sherman, yet the length of frontage was so great
that the investment could hardly be considered a very strong one. Besides these
40,000 besieged in Vicksburg, there was
Gen. J. E. Johnson at Canton and Jackson
with an army of from 45,000 to 50,000 men
supposed by General Grant to be ready to
assail his rear at any moment, and thus
compel him to raise the siege. Therefore,
Sherman was ordered to storm the fortifications on the right, if possible, on the 19th.

This was gallantly and furiously attempted, but it resulted in a failure, because of the strength, naturally and artificially, of the enemy's position. Besides, he had a sufficient number of troops to man every point and line of his whole plan of fortifications, in those 40,000 soldiers, because their lines being within ours, were of necessity, much shorter, and their base of supplies and supports much more accessible. The army nor the generals were by no means discouraged by this failure, and General Grant hoped to take Vicksburg with the men he had, in order that he could at once turn his compliments to the care of Johnson, and thus clear out the secession element in this section of its strength, without calling the much needed forces in other parts of the great struggle. He therefore ordered a general charge on all parts of the line by all of his divisions, on the 22nd of May at 10 o'clock A. M. precisely. Generals Mc. Pherson, Sherman and Mc. Clernand sat their watches with Grant's, and punctually on time the assault was made; the men carrying scaling ladders in case they could be used with advantage.

Although the assault was desperately made and frequently repeated, yet the position of the enemy was too strong to be thus taken, and therefore this second general movement on Vicksburg was destined to be ranked with the first one, although we gained several advantageous positions. But our loss was fearful in killed and wounded, and hence the price we paid for the advantages we gained was far too high to wish to see another bid in the same direction.

Gen. Grant therefore called for reinforcements, and immediately began to sap and mine the fortifications in front of Mc. Pherson, preparatory to a grand "blow up," as soon as the work could be accomplished.

For more than a year, or since the advance on Corinth, the spade had played but an inferior note in the grand drama of this part of the rebellion: but now its uses were to be added to the weapons of war, and the object of its mission was "the black fort," which was immediately in front of General Logan's Division. The sapping and mining, therefore by right, belonged to his force to accomplish; and manfully did they set themselves to the difficult task before them. The mine was completed on the 24th day of June, it being just one month since it was commenced. Orders had been circulated to assault the works at the mine immediately after the explosion.

The mine penetrated to a very few feet

of the rebel side of the walls of the fort;
and it was the current rumor then that six
barrels of powder were deposited in the
vault. At 4 o'clock P. M. the the troops
were stationed, and all waiting for the igni-
tion of of the fuze. Some delay occurred,
and the mine was not exploded until near
5 c'clock. I stood about 250 yards distant
from the mine at the time of the explosion,
and felt the tremble of the shock very per-
ceptably at the moment. The noise was a
dull heavy thud, unlike any thing I ever
heard, and then a column of smoke, dirt
and dust ascended full 100 feet in the air.
It had scarcely settled before the familliar
sound of heavy musketry was heard in the
partial breach made by the explosion. Our
men gained an inside position and held it
for over two hours, but finding it possessed
no advantages commensurate with the cost
of holding it; and therefore the soldiers were
withdrawn, and another failure experienced.
Logan's division lost in this assault twenty-
five killed and eighty-five wounded.

Six men of the enemy were blown over
the breastworks and into our lines, all of
whom were either killed or mortally wounded
except one, a negro named "Abe," of whom
a good picture and fine description were
given in Harper's Pictorial Weekly soon

thereafter. Abe was badly bruised, and for some days I thought his chances to live very doubtful. He fell in soft ground, and evidently on the back part of his head and shoulders, as there were the most serious injuries. In about a week he could walk, and Logan wanted to see him. He was therefore produced, and the following dialogue took place.

L. Are you the man that was blown up?

A. Yes Sa.

L. What is your name?

A. Abe Sa.

L. What did you mean by fighting us who are the friends of the black man?

A. I wuzent fitn you'ns Sa.

L. Then what were you doing?

A. I was blong to Capm ———— Sa.

L. But did you not have a gun and shoot at the Yanks?

A. No Sa! fo God, no Sa!

L. Where were you at the time of the explosion?

A. Mighty close under the breastworks, sleepn in the shade.

L. What did you let them blow you up for? why did you not hold on to something?

A. I dun gone hel on a bush Sa, but it blowd up too.

L. How high did you go?

A. Dun know Sa, speck bout 3 or 4 mile.

[Exit Abe, some ahead.]

Poor Abe was the dumbest mortal I ever saw. I had him for my servant for near a month after his recovery, but failed to get him to comprehend the regularity of any of my wants. To have invented such unsophisticated stupidity as he constantly exercised much transcended the capacity of any human being.

On the 20th of June another mine was ignited in the site of the former one; but it was of insignificant importance, and was not followed by any determined effort on the part of the soldiery to breach the enemy's works.

At about this time General Grant ordered all the mounted artilery to open upon the enemy, commencing at 5 A. M. and to cease at 8. giving 3 hours of bombardment. We had over 1200 pieces in position, and the explosions of artilery during those three hours averaged over 80 per minute. And these 14,400 explosions were from shot and shell all meaning death and destruction for those against whom they were sent.

It was very hot and dry, and many persons predicted rain would fall as a consequence of this bombardment; but for once, although the mouths of 1200 cannon were opened and thundered their deep toned emphasis, yet the clouds responded not.

On the 1 ts of July another bombardment in like manner from the whole line was executed on the doomed city and fortifications. All these efforts at destroying the enemy did but small service, as they would lie under cover of their bomb-proof breast-works, and the citizens had dug caves in the hillsides, to which on the first appearance of danger they would betake themselves like rats when Tom goes mousing.

General Grant now began to arrange for a desperate assault to be concluded on the 6 th of July. He pressed all his wagons in the service of hauling ammunition from the Yazoo landing, and every gun was to be supplied with 250 rounds of ammunition; the Infantry with 100 rounds to each man. The Cavalry, well mounted, equipped and supplied, were constantly scouring the country, looking after the wily Johnson and his forces who were hovering around our flanks and rear. Pemberton, from within Vicksburg, was trying to send word to Gen. Johnson, and General Grant captured two bearers of dispatches with their documents in cypher, who were seeking to pass our lines either to or from Vicksburg. Doubtless Pemberton knew of the grand preparations transacting to assault him, and conjectured that it would come off as a grand 4th of July celebration on that day, now only three days distant. He felt his inferiority, and called a council of his generals to consult upon what to do under the gloomy prospect. It being decided to capitulate under the best terms obtainable, the White Flag of Truce was raised upon the rebel works at many points, on the 3rd of July, and firing ceased on both sides.

This cessation of firing produced a very peculiar and anxious stillness — a sanctified Sunday had fallen upon us in mid-week — and every mouth and ear was asking and listening for the next announcement

The manner of the surrender. the participants in the negotiations, the place and the correspondence, are all familliar subjects of history.

The ever memorable

FOURTH DAY OF JULY 1863

was celebrated by a Triumphal Entry of General Grant's Army of the Tennessee, into the City of Vicksburg by three columns each headed by their respective corps commanders, from the Center, Right and Left. General Logan's Division was honored by being placed in the advance of the Center under the gallant Mc. Pherson, in the grand day of national glory — more effulgently glorious now than ever before to every participant of this crowning achievement which gave 36,600 prisoners of war as trophies to reward the valor of those who bore aloft in the dread thunders of all these battles and assaults, sieges and blood the Stars and Stripes of the Union Army in the great struggle for National life and right.

Officers and men, dressed in their best uniforms, marched to marshal music and the rusty uncombed butternut colored rebels behold the power and personnel of the "mud-sills and hireling yankees" who had so constantly conquered them. The day was clear and extremely warm, the dust deep and stinking with the accumulated filth (for they could not scavenger the city during the siege,) and altogether the exercise was very uncomfortable to the actors, except in the satisfaction of being conquerors in a series of contests which penetrated to the vitals of the rebellion in the South West.

We took up our quarters in Vicksburg and commenced paroling prisoners, attending to sanitary improvements, overhauling confederate stores, hospitals, ammunition, ordnance and supplies. General Logan was placed in command of the Post of Vicksburg, and I as Surgeon-in-Chief of his Division, commenced my Official Reports of all the surgical proceedings of the Third Division of the Seventeenth Army Corps, from the day we left Milikin's Bend to the time when Pemberton surrendered Vicksburg and his army therein besieged.

This labor was, with the current daily duties, an immense work for me. I had but two clerks, and to give an idea of what we accomplished, to satisfy the insatiate demands of a coxcomb and thief who held the office of Corps Medical Director, I will say that from July 6th to Oct. 21st we consumed 10 reams of paper in my office. I have reason to believe that my Reports never reached Washington; because they were full and as explicit as it was possible in my capacity to make them, and probably were too much so for their preservation, as in being transmitted they had to pass through the slippery fingers of this corps director. I do not wonder, judging from my own case, and knowing that other Division Surgeons had a similar routine to fulfill, that the Surgeon in charge of the Medical Archives in Washington, Dr. Brinton, after a two years trial, rose from his labors and reported that the heaps of medical communications at the Surgeon General's Office was simply a mass of confused rubbish out of which no valuable data could be gathered. But he, as much as any man in the service, had issued or caused to be issued those very orders and regulations for gathering exactly this same "mass of confused rubbish," which every surgeon knew beforehand would not meet the end desired. The plain and humilliating truth is, that our Surgeon General was but an exceedingly dishonest and thoroughly incompetent man; and the Surgical History of the Rebellion is not what it should be more from these causes than any or all other causes combined. Surgeon General Hammond was court-marshaled and cashiered for incompetence and dishonesty. My friend Major General R. J. Oglesby, was commissioned President of the Court which found Dr. Hammond deeply guilty of all the charges preferred against him. I am frank to acknowledge that I felt great satisfaction at the finding of this court in the case of Hammond for his deceptive trickery in the case of my appointed examination for Surgeon of Volunteers which should in good faith have taken place Dec. 29. 1862 at Washington, as previously stated.

On the 21. of Oct. 1863. I obtained a leave of absence to visit my home, and on arriving there found my little family happy in the new society of our sixth child and fourth daughter,

Miss Lillian Hattie Trowbridge,

who was born July 17th 1863. She was our "war baby," but her genial nature shows none of the hostile spirit of the times in her composition. She was a beautiful blue-eyed blonde, strong and healthy, and over three months old when I first saw her.

And now that I have conveyed myself home on leave of absence, after having past the great campaigns just delineated, and found my cheerful babes and their fond mother in good health, and exceedingly happy in giving their soldier husband and father a cordial welcome such as none but they could give, I will pass some of those two weeks in recording a few

INCIDENTS OF THE CAMPAIGN

not mentioned in the previous pages. To have done so would have broken the descriptive chain of greater events.

The siege bestowed many of these minor incidents worthy of mention, and doubtless I shall forget many of them, for every day almost, gave us some novelty exciting to our mess. I recollect of sitting at our dinner table, in the rear of Vicksburg, when a shell descended and alighted just by the fire on which our frugal fare was cooked, and not three rods distant when it exploded. It did no damage, only it was observed that our apetites were not very craving thereafter. At another time Dr Denison, while sitting in a secure place, as he thought, was struck by a spent musket ball on the knee, which resulted in so severe a case of inflammation of the joint (Synovitis) as to endanger his life for several days.

One day Lt. Pearse and I left our business tents to go to dinner. In going there it was necessary, to be safe, to pass down a hollow and up another, a distance of a mile or more thus going around a hill to reach our mess-table — the same by which the shell exploded the day before — It was extremely hot, and to pass over the hill permitted us to reach the mess in about a quarter of a mile. This hill was in full view of the enemy, and about 500 yards distant. We proposed to go over the hill at full speed and save the long dusty and hot ride around the hollows. We drew cuts to see who should go first, the chance falling on Lt. Pearse. He was riding a stubby old horse and we were following an irregular cow path up the hill-side. He was in the rear, and as we were gaining the brow of ridge where we could see the rebs, Pearse put spurs to his horse and was passing me to lead in the chase when I reached down and caught Stubby by the tail and cried out "ho!" and stopped his horse by a tree round which Pearse would have turned in the instant. Just then a ball struck the tree, and had it not been for my buffoonry in stopping the horse that ball would have certainly wounded or killed my good friend Pearse. We concluded that the valleys had many attractions and forthwith went to see them.

I was busily engaged, one day, writing at a desk in my tent, when Lt. Pearse, from his tent, called out, "Trowbridge! come quick!" I arose and stepped towards him when a musket ball struck the desk ranging just right to have hit me in the center of the back. Pearse had seen me very busy and thought to annoy me by a little pleasantry and hence his imperious call and the saving of my life as the result of his facetiousness.

I had no truer friend than H. N. Pearse in the whole army, and I had a chance to return this saving compliment by gaining his final discharge from the service, when to have remained longer was almost a sure promise of death.

Major Stallbrand, Chief of Artilery on Gen. Logan's Staff, had a shell burst in his tent while he was in it, perfectly demolishing every thing but himself, he stepping out of the midst of the ruins and swearing that if he was not one of the best christians in the world he would have been killed outright. But when he discovered a find gold watch, a present from his father, totally ground to atoms I thought his christianity the most vehement and demonstrative I had ever seen.

I think his escape, unharmed as he was, one of the greatest wonders of all the curious things I ever saw.

GARRISONING VICKSBURG.

My leave of absence expiring, I again kissed my wife and babies good bye, to join the forces still in Vicksburg. On returning we found camp life very monotonous, and only had it broken by few incidents worthy of record until my time of service expired on the 25. of the following July.

We marched once to Monroe La. and once to Canton with quite a little battle again on or near the old Champion's Hill battle ground. Then Gen. Sherman started on the 3. day of Feb. 1864 on his march to the Sea from Vicksburg. This march reached no further than Meridian, Miss. and resulted in destroying the railroad from Jackson to Meridian which was, as I thought, well done but the enemy had cars running over it in two months time afterwards. This failure to go further resulted from Gen. W. S. Smith who was to leave Memphis Feb. 1st and to join Sherman at Meridian. Smith was grossly whipped; and hence we returned to Vicksburg. Gen. Sherman then started his great scheme from Atlanta Ga. After we had returned to Vicksburg, the 8th Ill. Inf. Veteranized, or reelinsted for the close of the war; and for this act of patriotism they were allowed a 30 days furlough at their homes. This occurred during the month of April 1864, and the regiment of veterans took their scars and bullet beaten banners back to show them and themselves to the admiring multitudes who thronged to see the remnant of the first regiment which had offered its services to the country from the patriotic state of Illinois.

The City of Decatur gave the regiment a dinner at the Revere House, and the ladies of Springfield gave another similar entertainment at a public hall in that city. This last mentioned affair presented several features of worthy note. At this feast the Ajutant General of the State of Illinois presided, and made a speech in which he gave the marches, battles, sieges, campaigns &c. in minute accuracy, in which this Regt. had been engaged, and paid the officers and men the highest compliment for " being the bravest among the brave before the enemy, and before the ladies and society in general patrons of gentility." He told of the exact number of official promotions; the number of days the regiment had been under fire, being 104 days; the numder of men slain on the battle field being 101; the number dying from wounds while in General Hospital and at home on furlough, being 68; the number dying in the regimental hospital from wounds and disease, being 28; the number sent to gen. hos. and dying there of disease, being 37; the number discharged on surgeons certificate of disability from disase and wounds, being 46 and 70 respectively. He also stated another fact, that this regiment sent less men to the General Hospital than any other regiment from Illinois; had had more men slain in battle and fewer deaths in the regimental hospital than any regiment in the service from any state of the Union. After saying these things he turned upon me while sitting upon the platform before the large audience and said "there Ladies and Gentlemen, is the man who is guilty of bringing about all these sanitary results. The Colonel, J. A. Sheetz, with whom I have just been talking, has told me all about that man, and I now take great pleasure in exposing him to you."

My modesty was sorely tried by these compliments, and is now again in writing them, but he who squanders time by reading autobiographies must expect to meet the like, or there would be none written.

We were constantly hearing of Shermans preparations for his march on Atlanta, while we were at home, and was informed that our regiment would constitute a part of that great enterprise; and all the men were eager for the campaign. Our camp equipage was ordered up to Cairo to meet us there, but orders came, ultimately for us to return to garrison Vicksburg. We were disgusted at this turn of our fortunes, almost feeling ourselves disgraced, and our gallant officers hinted as much, but were told that some reliable force must be left to hold Vicksburg and so we had to submit.

On our return to Vicksburg, while passing Island No. 10 we were fired into by a thick headed dunce who had been left there to garrison the Island. A 12 lb. shell striking the bow of the boat just at the water-line, doing but little damage. We rounded too, and asked what was wanted, when we were informed by the officer as follows: "I command this Island, and shall allow no boat to pass without a written permit from me." On being asked for an exhibit of his orders for such a proceeding he said he had none, but he intended to enforce the regulation. Colonel Sheetz then told him that he was going to proceed on his voyage without observing his arrogant orders, and if molested, he must take the consequences. Duncy seeing that this meant serious work, said, "all right, go ahead!" and thus ended our insolent hailing.

Our duty in garrisoning Vicksburg was a tedious, monotonous, uneventful one, and all were glad when it ended. The time of enlistment was to expire on the 25th day of July following, and those who had not veteranized were waiting anxiously for the day to arrive when they should become civil citizens at their homes once more. The men and officers often complimented me by very earnestly soliciting that I should remain with them, and yet they knew and felt that I had not been fairly dealt with by the higher authorities, in not being permitted to pass my examination for promotion as a Medical Inspector in December 1862, when invited to do so by Inspector General T.

F. Perley, and prevented by the dishonest conduct of Surg. Gen. Hammond. As a sample of these flattering testimonials, the following extract from a letter, the author of which is still unknown to me, published in the Decatur Gazette, Nov. 17, 1863, is an instance.

"All who know any-thing of our history, know that the 8. Illinois has had less sickness and fewer deaths by desease, by at least one half, than any other regiment in the army of the Tennessee. For this, our Surgeons deserve the credit. Our tried friend Dr. Trowbridge, stil lremains with us and probably will, since it is quite obvious that officers who are honest in the discharge of their duties do not receive just appreciation, in some instances. It is not denied Dr. Trowbridge passed an excellent examination, and was the first Surgeon commissioned from the state; that he was the most successful army Surgeon ever on duty at Cairo, and that he cured more bad cases than any Surgeon in this army; but as he does not belong to any particular clique, he still remains a Regimental Surgeon, the same as he started. These things are wonderfully strange, but true."

In fact these compliments were varied; as at the reorganization of the regiment as veterans, I was frequently importuned by the men to become Colonel of the regiment. But this I could not do in justice to the truly brave and highly efficient officers who had borne the Heat and burthen of the day, who were my good friends and much better posted in military tactics than I.

Although my term of service, expiring on the 25 th day of July as it did, and all the non-veterans were mustered out of the service at Springfield Illinois, yet they said that I might still be wanted, and therefore my discharge was held in abeyance until the 28 th day of August 1864, when I received an honorable discharge from the service; having served two appointments comprising three years and four months.

Thus ends my military career. And in leaving the army, I bid farewell to some of the best friends I ever had, probably to never to see them again on earth.

May peace and prosperity follow their footsteps, and a long life be theirs to enjoy in the land their patriotic valor contributed to save from the ravages of ruthless rebels.

DOMESTIC LIFE AGAIN.

I had entertained doubts as to whether I should feel contented in settling down to my former professional habits in the practice of medicne; but on arriving at home, I formed a copartnership with my old friend Dr. W. J. Chenoweth, and at once recieved calls and patronage far outstripping my expectations. This copartnership dated from the day of my being mustered out of the service, or rather, when I should have been mustered out on the 25. day of July 1864.

I gave more especial attention to the surgical department, while Dr C. turned his attentions to the obstetrical branch of the profession, and thus we carried two specialities with the large general practice which came to our office. These engrossing labors occupied my time so fully that I had no opportunity to become disgusted with the routine of domestic practice or to draw invidious comparisons between it and the Surgeon's service in the army. I was often called upon to go long distances, to perform surgical operations, and patients often came from other states to consult me. I will record here three cases of my practice, although there were many others of equal importance and merit which came to our care for treatment.

Case 1. A little girl of 4 years, daughter of Mr. Constance living in the N. W. part of our County was kicked by a horse in the right temple, crushing in the skull bones most frightfully. The badly mutillated little one was found in the stable, lying in a pool of blood, and having convulsions every few moments. Dr. C. and I were called to see the little sufferer and made a night of it before we reached the house and finished our operation. On examining the wound I found a long fragment of bone loose, and on attempting to remove it, opened the Median Meningial Artery which had been ruptured, but which had, for some cause unknown to us, ceased to bleed. Other contiguous bones were much depressed, causing in our judgment, the convultions. I attempted to raise these bones and succeeded admirably at the same time the hemorrhage ceased from the Median Meningial. We watched carefully and anxiously for a recurrence of the hemorrhage when reaction should set in, if that favourable symptom should come. Of course we expected inflammation of the brain to follow the injury, and our prognosis was unfavourable as to the final result of the case. We saw the reaction come up, and no bleeding followed. We concluded that the torn extremity of the artery had been accidentally caught between the broken edges of the bones as we brought them in their proper position, and thus the compression of the artery was an arrest of the chances of recurrence of hemorrhage. And at day-light we left for home, little expecting a favourable result of the case. Mr. Constance asked our bill, and we told him we had been operating upon an almost hopeless case, and did not feel like charging full fee on such; that the fee would be $50, but under the circumstances we would charge $30, and if the case recovered we would claim the other $20. In about three weeks Mr. Constance called at our office and paid the $20 in question, and feeling as greatful and happy in doing so as any man I ever saw, saying at the time that his little daughter was well and all her faculties perfect. She had no inflammation to speak of, nor other untoward symptoms, after we left her, nor had he to call for the local aid of doctors residing near by.

Case 2. I received a telegram one evening to go to Pana, 34 miles on the R. R. South of Decatur, to operate upon the son of Mr. Humphries, who had been horribly mutillated by the cars passing over him at

5. P. M. that evening. The R. R. Co.
ordered an engine and tender to be placed
at my service and soon I was en route for
the scene of the accident. Several of the Pana
physicians were waiting for me, and on
reaching the bed-side of the wounded boy,
found him in a collapsed state from the severe shock and loss of blood. The car had
lacerated his left leg and thigh frightfully,
so much so that when the lacerations were
closed by sutures and the seams measured
their total length was found to be 33 inches.
But there were no bones broken in this
extremity. We dressed these wounds of the
leg and thigh, and then waited for reaction
before going further, for this was but the
small part of his injuries. The car-wheel
had passed over the whole length of his left
arm crushing bones and flesh from the hand
to the shoulder. At 9. A. M. of the next
day we succeeded in establishing a partial
reaction of the circulation and determined
to operate at once by giving Chloroform and
removing the arm at the shoulder joint, by
Baron Larre's method. I called the deeply
distressed parents aside and told them just
what I had to fear and what to hope for.

The fears were that he would die under
the operation; and there was nothing for
which to hope without the operation being

at once performed. Suffice it to say that I came out of this interview with my feelings very much excited by the agonizing anxiety of the fond parents, but immediatly mailed my emotions with a surgeons iron-clad armor of resolution and self control and ended the operation in less than 4 minutes thereafter.

This young man recovered after a lingering confinement of over 3 months, and always appered grateful for the services I had rendered, though bashful, awe-struck and reticent in my presence, nor have I ever been able to cultivate any intimacy with him whatever.

Case 3. Private Benson of the 116. Regt. Ill. Inf. was struck with a fragment of shell on the side of his head, depressing the bones of the right temple very much.

This occured at or near Atlanta Ga. when Sherman was battering the confederacy at that place. Surgeon Barnes of that regiment saw the case 3 or 4 days after the patient had received the injury, and sent him to Gen. Hospital. He was not expected to live, and was subsequently sent to St. Louis whence he was discharged from the service on Surgeon's Certificate of Disability. He never received any surgical treatment, because he could not be recovered from the ground on which he fell for the 2. or 4. days after being wounded, and at which time Surgeon Barnes first saw him. The comfortable condition of the patient, considering the gravity of the injury, induced the Surgeons to let him alone and hence the surgical non-intervention. Eighteen months after receiving his injury, while working on his farm, at husking corn, which required much stooping down, he was seized with a violent convulsion. His friends sent for a physician living in a little village close by who visited him but did nothing but advise quiet and no labor. In two weeks he had another epileptic attack more violent, and these convulsions came on more frequent and severe until he had them every hour, when he sent for me to come and see him.

Knowing that Dr. Barnes was his surgeon in the army and then a practitioner in Decatur, I asked why Dr. B. was not called? They told me that he had been, but would not go, giving as his excuse that he did no surgery and had no instruments. I sent my compliments to Dr. B. saying my instruments were at his service and myself as assistant should he desire my aid. But he refused to go, and Dr. Chenoweth and myself went at once, fully prepared to operate if the case admitted. We found Mr. Benson insenisble, having the most violent epileptic convulsions every few minutes. We examined the case and decided to trephine the depressed bones. After an operation lasting two hours and three quarters, and having removed three pieces of depressed bone by boring as many times through the skull; we began to discover that the tendency to convulsions was subsiding. We closed the apperture of the skull with the flesh flaps, we had laid aside in order to bare the skull for the trephine, when this simple pressure reproduced the convulsions. This showed us plainly that we had removed all the offending bones and now, all that remained was to dispose of this soft pressure by loosening it. This proving true we gave directions for future treatment to the local doctor and had the pleasure of seeing Mr. Benson in after times injoying good health and sound faculties.

After arriving home from the army, I bought and sold real estate in Decatur, doubling my resources several times over; although the capital started out with was but a small one, and therefore these doublings still were not much in the line of thousands. Yet I realized more from this source than from the labors of my profession.

The winter and spring of 1866 was a sore trial for the lungs of Mrs. Tlowbridge, and

I began to fear the consequences would become serious in the extreme. She was attended with very poor health for a year, frequently taking backsets after partial recoveries, until the Spring of 1867, when her condition became very alarming to me. I dared not exhibit my anxiety, and often had her case examined by my medical friends, always as if by accident or coincidence, so as not to arouse her fears or cause her to bestow upon herself any thought or concern whatever. She began to have a deep hollow cough, was poor and emaciated, and although a tall large lady, yet she weighed less than 120 lbs.; whereas her usual weight was 10 or 15 lbs. more. I had contemplated removing to some more congenial and healthy climate should her case demand it, when a circumstance occurred which gave me the desired change with all the good results we so much wanted. These circumstances were as follows: A music master's little boy was taken sick and I was called to treat him, which required several visits before the little fellow became convalescent. On visiting our little patient one day, I met the father and mother sitting with their recovering child beside them, playing for his amusement on brass instruments. Mrs. Smith (for such was her name) became flushed by the effort, and the exercise to the lungs was such as to attract my attention, and occasioned some thought on my part, which resulted in my making him a proposition to teach a band of ladies, music on the brass horns. Mr S. cheerfully caught the proposition, and his wife said she would join if Mrs. Trowbridge would. I guaranteed Mrs. Trowbridge's cooperation and that of my daughter Ada, then 14 years of age and a fair performer on the piano. Mrs. Trowbridge readily consented to become a member of the band on condition that it should be a private affair. She solicited Sherrif Bear's daughter to be a companion for Ada, and soon the band was in successful operation composed of 8 members. They made extraordinary progreys, and I perceived that Mrs Trowbridge's cough had entirely disappeared within three weeks time from when she commenced to practice. She blew a B flat Alto, and gained a good apetite and flesh from the start. I became enthusiastic for the band and encouraged them by all the persuasive powers I possessed to give public exhibitions. I furnished a horse and band-wogon, bought new german silver instrewments for my wife and daughter, a large bass drim for my sone Charlie, then only 11 years old.

The band was organized in the latter part

of June 1867, and played for the public, at
a Base Ball Tournament, given at Decatur,
in the following Fall; and at the County
Fair, which took place two weeks later.
At this Fair Captain Mc. Donald, commanding the fine river Steamboat called the
M. S. Mepham of St. Louis, hearing the
band playing at the Fair Ground, sought
an introduction to the members, and invited
them to take an excursion to New Orleans
on his boat. This invitation was accepted on
condition that I would go with them.
Although this would subtract much from my
practice, yet I saw that it would be an additional source of remedy to Mrs Trowbridge
by giving her change of living as well as of
climate; and for this I promptly consented
to go. We went and had a merry holi-day
for two months, and when Mrs. Trowbridge
returned from this excursion she was entirely restored. And then I knew, for she told
me, that she was just as conscious as I was
of her precarious hold on health and life for
the year and more just past.

The band then laid aside their instruments
not giving a blast upon a horn for two years.
when the same symptoms again began to
show themselves and a return to the horns
again restored her, and I have little fear at
present of weak lungs in her case.

Before trying the wind-instrument treatment for Mrs. Trowbridge, she had accompanied me on a visit to my relatives in the state of Indiana, and tarried there while I attended a meeting of the American Medical Association, that year held at Cincinnati, of which I had been a member since 1854. This short journey did but little service for her health, and my anxiety was more arroused than appeased by the result of the visit.

But all praises be ascribed unto the horns for her recovery!

When on our excursion to New Orleans we stopped one night at

NEW MADRID, MISSOURI,

because the Mississippi River was so low that we could not run during the nights. The Captain had sent out invitations to the young gentlemen of the place to bring in their ladies and have a dance on his boat, as he had done the two nights previously at Cape Giradeau and Cairo respectively. This invitation being accepted, at about 8 o'clock one or two couples had arrived on board, when the wharf-boat master came to the captain and said there were some very suspicious characters in town that day, and he would advise him to close his bar for the night to prevent dificulty. Captain Mc. Donnald said he would do so cheerfully, and yet he did not think anybody would molest him. He turned to me and said "Dr, please to act as Captain for me for a half hour and receive the guests as they come in, as I want to go on shore," I said "all right," and he turned to go off the boat. We were in the "Social Hall" at the time, and just then the darkey barber came to us saying to the Captain that there were in his barber-shop 5 robbers planning to capture and burn the boat. Capt. Mc. D. laughed at the barber and sent him to his shop again, but said to me that he would not go on shore, and therefore would not trouble me with any of his commissions. At this we were joined by a drunken man from the barber-shop. This somewhat arroused my suspicions but I turned to my state room, which was at the extreme end of the boat, and having been up late the two nights previously, laid myself down upon my berth. I had not lain there more than 2 or 3 minutes when I heard 3 pistol shots at the forward end of the boat, and great confusion of voices, tumbling of furniture and slamming of doors. I sprang to my feet and looked in the direction of the disturbance and saw the Capt. desperately fighting with a man who had

the Captain down and was trying to use a
bright instrument on him which I thought
to be a knife. Although there were 65 male
passengers on board and but a moment before were in the "Main Hall," yet now not
a soul of them could be seen there but these
two men engaged in mortal combat. I dashed down the hall to the assistance of Captain
Mc. Donald and reached him just in time to
seize the ruffian as he was dealing the Cap.
a violent stroke with his pistol, which I had
mistaken for a knife the moment before. I
caught the brute by the hair and gave such
a violent jerk that Capt. Mc. Donald obtained complete power over him, and planted
some of the finest pugilistic shots ever invented in various telling places about his
"mug." He appeared very loth to discon-
tinue this exercise, until I felt sure he would
finish the fellow then and there if he did not
stop; when I mildly said to him "Captain,
for God's sake don't kill him!" Whereupon
he "ceased firing." Just then I saw a furious
looking fellow dashing up, and I thought
him to be another ruffian, and drew my pistol and made up my determination, that if
he turned out to be a foe and assaulted the
Captain, I would ram my weapon into his
face and blow out as many brains as a small
bored bullet could find in the short time it

might have to search for them as it passed through. But what he said and did convinced me effectually, that he intended to be a very efficient friend. He cried out, brandishing a cotton hook at the time, "Captain, let me have a hook at him!" and immediately caught the then limpsy villain by the under jaw with the sharp hook and snaked him to the head of the stairs where he commenced the most active and liberal application of brogan bruising I had ever seen.

Brigand No. 2, now being discovered, he darted for the door and met the first Engineer, a low, heavy set, square man, who planted a hard bony fist so snugly in his face that he laid sprawling at the mercy of another active pair of square toed stogas which lifted him clear of the deck at each oft repeated application.

Brigand No. 3, not liking the situation, nor the door out of which his two confederates had passed, started to escape at the opposite door, and was fortunate in meeting the Mate, Mr. Cogsdell, whose profession had long since rendered him a proficient in knocking down "roustabouts," and he just now extended it so as to include this needy biped. I did not see the subsequent disposition of No. 3, but learned that he was thrown from the forecastle to a barge along side, a distance of 12 to 14 feet, and permitted to select any miscellaneous mode of alighting which might turn up. The reason for me not witnessing the finale of this part of the tragedy was because

Brigand No. 4, appeared on the stage, retreating down the Main Hall to the middle of the boat where a door was situated, leading on to the guards, through which he dashed head foremost carrying the glass and panel as though they were made of the most fragile stuff. He gained the guards and jumped into the river; and no one had the hard heartedness to attempt to rob the cat-fishes of a dainty dish of mashed "Puke" in brandy sauce.

Brigand No. 5, ran upon Hurricane deck and to the rear end of the boat, followed by the 2d clerk with a cocked Derringer, and jumped into the river and swam ashore. Said 2d clerk failed to fire upon the flying foe although he snapped his pistol at him several times, but subsequently discovered that said Derringer was not loaded.

I then learned the following history of the commencement of the assault.

It appears that the villains had planned to get into a fight and in it to shoot the Captain and as many others as might be necessary to gain controll of the boat, to

sack and rob her of all they could take, and
then to burn her. When the Captain and
the Master of the Wharf-boat went forward
to close the bar, these five enterprising
Missourians were there at the bar. Captain
Mc. Donald said to the bar-tender "Jim,
close the bar and permit no one to have
liquor to night." These 5 men then drew
their pistols and said to Jim, "whiskey for
five or die!" Jim said as he set out the
glasses and grog, "Captain, what else can
I do?" At this the Captain stepped forward
and swept bottles and glasses on the floor,
when the leader turned with his pistol not
a foot from the heart of the Captain and
fired. Captain Mc. Donald knocked down
the pistol and the ball did no damage. Two
others of these murderous wretches fired at
the same time hitting no one, when the Captain closed with his assailant in the contest
of which I have before given the result. All
the passengers scrambled for their hiding
places and left the Captain as I said before
to the merciless ruffians, manifesting the
most abject cowardise. On looking over
the floor we saw blood had been profusely
knocked and kicked out of the would be
murderers, a large tuft of hair was the tro-
phy of my compliment to Brigand No 1.
and three pistols left by the retreating foe.

The gallant Captain was now in the undisputed possession of the field, and began to organize his pursuit of the enemy. He ordered his crew to "fall in," and called for volunteers from among the passengers. From the crew and these volunteers, he raised in about three minutes, a brave band of 13 men. With these he sallied on shore, and first paid a visit to the Mayor of the town, and demanded the arrest of the brigands, offering his dauntless 13 as marshals possie. But His Excellency told Captain Mc. Donald that they of New Madrid were perfectly at the mercy of these roughs, and although, with the aid of the force offered, the would be murderers might probably be apprehended, but then these five were as but a drop in the bucket, and their confederates would descend upon the town as soon as the Mepham would leave the place and His Satanic Highness could only invent for them to execute all manner of outrages upon the defenseless citizens.

We saw the situation, and assuming all responsibilities, started in pursuit on our own account, Striking at once in the direction of the suspected lurking place of the gorrillas, we were passing a lone house, and two of us were on the floor under the awning when two pistol shots were fired at us by the enemy from the corner of the building and not ten feet distant from us. We rushed at the foe and stepping off the said platform, blinded by the flash of their pistols, I fell to the ground and Capt. Mc. Donald exclaimed " My God! Dr. Trowbridge is killed." "No" said I, "not hit, I only fell. Capt. take half of the men and go after them and I will take the other half and go to head them off at the next block." The men all ran with Mc. Donald and I started to head them off, as I said, not knowing that I was going alone. At the next corner I was shot at by two scamps from the opposite side of the street, when they broke ranks and fled. I could see them indistinctly in the dark but fired at them twice, bringing a lusty yell, on the last fire, of "Oh! my God!" At this moment I heard the other party arresting men at the point I had intended to have met them. These men were a party of innocent wood-choppers and were promptly released. We returned to the Mepham, supposing that all hostilities had ceased.

This was at 9 o'clock P. M. At eleven they came back and fired 15 or 20 shots into the boat wounding three men slightly. At one A. M. they fired 5 or 10 shots more from on shore, but did no damage, and at 3 A. M. again they gave us a volly and fled leaving us to go on our way in peace.

We learned, during the night, that these rascals had caught the Captain of the "J. M. White" on shore, tied and robbed him and his steamboat, and then set the vessel on fire, after turning it adrift on the river. Also that the "Mariah Denning" only escaped their villainy by cutting her head-lines and steaming out into the river leaving her staging. And these acts of vandalism had occurred but two or three weeks previously to their attack on us. But their experiences with the Mepham stopped all other assaults on the navigation passing New Madrid. When we returned from New Orleans we had freight to put off at New Madrid, and arrived there at about 7 o'clock P. M., but were prepared for any emergency that might present. No molestation was offered however, and we then learned that three of the scamps were still suffering patients of a certain doctor of the place, but recovering, two from contusions, bruises, and a broken arm and one from a pistol shot in the back. Brigand No. 1, had the temerity to send word to Capt. Mc. Donald to send him his pistol .a fine silver plated one, but the Captain sent him word that he must come after it himself, that he would be passing there often, and would be, only too well pleased to attend to him whenever or wherever he should meet him.

EXCURSION WITH THE EDITORS.

On the 12th. of October 1867, about 250 Editors, representing nearly that number of periodicals, took an excursion starting at Chicago and reaching as far west as to 25 miles west of Juelsburg on the Pacific Railroad, and returning to the same city of commencement. I was solicited to go along as surgeon of the expedition, as they very well knew the services of a surgeon might be called in requisition. This was a grand cavalcade of sensationalists on a rampage. We occupied eight Pullman sleeping cars, one baggage car, one dining car and two for saloon and stoes, to compose our train. The roads gave us our own time, and a free way, and we made a grand sensation wherever we went. The history of this excursion was so many times written and published by those editors, so extravagantly and so diversifiedly described in every imaginable way and manner, so many truths and untruths told about it, told in plain and spread-eagle English and in Chocktaw even, that I do not intend to worry my readers with a very lengthy detail of the circumstances connected

with it, although I never in all my life saw
so many semi-note-worthy sights and transactions crouded into 14 consecutive days.
We had a crazy one horse band of music
in grog; George Francis Train; buffalo
beef; alkaline water and cholera symptoms
from mixing too freely these incompatible
elements; Ossian E. Dodge to spout extem-
pore poetical filth and Frank Lombard to
sing it; a buffalo hunt at Ft. Kearny and
killed 19 buffalo bulls; a war-dance with
Big Mouth; big dinners at Omaha, Conucil
Bluffs and Chicago; a run of 139 miles,
from Julesburg to Ft. Kearny, in just two
hours to a minute; saw the workmen at the
end of track laying the day they laid 5 miles
and 9 rods of track in one day; heard Train
make a speech in what he said was good
Japanees gibberish, and saw him kick sand
in the faces of Big Mouth and all his cowardly braves; saw the Platt River with its
ten thousand islands; saw more praire dogs
than this whole army of editors could count
in a month; shot wolves, deer, antelope,
mule rabbits, praire dogs, and any other dog
that dared to present himself while the train
was in motion; saw a Methodist preacher
shoot six rounds from his carbine at some
oxen thinking they were buffalo; heard Big
Mouth display his Indian eloquence by beg-

ging tin trinkets of his pale-faced friends; heard "Kansas Bill" with his tribe of "bull whackers;" saw Dr. Hayden's exploring party and had a long and very interesting conversation with him; saw a grave-yard of many graves of which it was said that not a single dead man laid there who had died a natural death; saw a Julesburg gambling house with all its horribly disgusting appurtenances, of which the town of about 5,000 inhabitants was principally composed; heard the Mayor of Julesburg welcome those 250 editors by telling them he hoped they would make themselves free and easy but in order to do that safely in Julesburg it was necessary to strip as for the ring, to buckle on pistols and knives "and then go in;" and in fine, saw more drunken material in men and benzine whisky and less drunkenness than I had expected could be found in any 250 "ink slingers," as they styled themselves, in the whole United States, and all to get home safe and sound, without any accident, and look on arriving there as if they were the most innocent and deeply persecuted people on earth.

Now that is a short synopsis of the great Editorial Excursion: each item of which might be enlarged, extended and embellished with much interesting minutiæ, but I decline, resigning in favor of all the American Newspapers of those dates for full and elaborate detail.

LITTLE FREDDIE.

On the 20th day of July 1868, we had born unto us a beautiful little boy, who never breathed a breath of life on earth. We laid our angel babe beside his brother Lewis Edwin, twin souls in Immortality. We named him Freddie, and registered him in The Good Book of the Family Record. On this occurrence Mrs. Trowbridge came very near to death's door, and I have again to record the saving intercession and assistance rendered by our very true friend Doctor W. J. Chenoweth. Her recovery was rapid and complete, showing the value of her thoroughly restored constitutional forces.

MEDICAL ASSOCIATIONS AND WHAT THE WRITER HAD TO DO WITH THEM.

I have purposely deferred alluding to my relations with the various medical societies with which I have been associated, in order to give the description of them in chronological conjunction.

Early in the year 1853, I had an inter-

view with all the medical gentlemen of the
Regular Profession of Macon County
Illinois, and it was agreed to call a meeting
of all such at my office, to take measures to
organize a County Medical Society in conformity with the rules of etiquette of the
American Medical Association, and of the
Illinois State Medical Society. We soon
succeeded in forming a lively society of a
few energetic and determined men, and I
was offered the presidency of it at its organization; but desiring that it should bear a
more dignified appearance by giving it an
honorable and venerable head, I declined
the proffered honor in favor of Dr. Joseph
King, who was unanimously elected, and I
accepted the more laborious office of Secretary & Treasurer.

I contributed several papers to this society, some of which may be found in the
Appendix of this work.

It is cheering to an autobiographer to
have an opportunity of making extracts
covering his subject, from the published
matter of others; and here I have the
chance of giving the history of my connection with this society, from the pen of
Dr. W. J. Chenoweth, in 1868, in an
address to that society on leaving its
presidential chair. He says;—

"Macon County Medical Society had its birth in the year 1853, and owes its existence to Dr. S. T. Trowbridge who alone urged its necessity and patiently pressed its claims on the profession. .... Dr. Trowbridge, my worthy predecessor, then as now. sought the field of surgery, which was not grudgingly withheld, but generously pressed on him by his competitors. Not having the same fear of inflicting pain, or probably being incited by an intense yearning for pre-eminence in this unoccupied field, he gave devoted attention to the few cases demanding surgical skill. But as these were too limited in number to admit of exclusive attention, and as the necessities of life must be met, he engaged in a general practice. Having a physical constitution of remarkable toughness. and almost ferruginous hardness, his labors were immense, and such as would not be courted by him now, although in the prime of life and in the vigor of health. I have known him, not unfrequently, to ride and drive as much as 400 miles in a single week, attending to the ordinary duties of the profession. Of his mental and moral qualities it ill becomes me to speak in detail, but I may be allowed to say that great intimacy will not permit me to adopt the adage , "familiarity breeds contempt."

I have already given him the credit of origi-
nating this society—I may add that to him
is due its life. After three years of struggle
it went down with the wreck of '57. He
again resurrected it in 1858. When the
war burst upon us in 1861, he was the first
physician in Illinois to offer his services,
as regimental surgeon, given to any physician in this State, or in the United States.
After remaining three years and three
months in the service and passing unharmed through all the great battles of Donelson,
(where he saved the life of John A. Logan,
our Congressman-at-Large,) Shiloh, Vicksburg, and Corinth, (at this last battle saving
to us and the country our present Governor
and townsman, R. J. Oglesby,) he returned
to find the society without an existence and
at once solicited aid to build it up a third
time. So that to him is due its present
prosperity.' [Hist. Macon Co. Med. Soc.]

ILLINOIS STATE MEDICAL SOCIETY.

I joined this society in 1854. In 1860
was appointed Chairman of the Committee
on Practical Medicine, but went to the war
in 1861, and did not report, although I had
my documents far on the way to completion,
and would have presented them on time,

there was no session of the society that year. In 1859 I was elected 2d Vice President and in 1866 was promoted another grade or to the 1st Vice Presidency and filled the chair during the session in consequence of the non-attendance of the President. In the year 1867, I was appointed Chairman of the Committee to memorialize the Legislature to pass laws prohibiting incompetent persons from practicing medicine and to grant dissecting privileges to medical men. I drew up the form of a law covering both of these heads, which were approved by the County and State Societies; but failed to induce our wise Solons in Springfield to make the law.

In 1868 I was elected President at the session held at Quincy, and presided there, and at Chicago in 1869. Thus had been shed upon me the highest honors in the gift of the medical fraternity of the Commonwealth of Illinois.

This meeting at Chicago gave the last interview I ever had with some of my best medical friends. Since then both Dr. H. Noble and Dr. S. W. Noble have died; and when I parted with them in Chicago, they said to me: "It is more than likely we may never meet again on earth. For you know the land to which you go is beset with many dangers; but God and our highest

regards be with you." The meeting will be
hence, far beyond the dark shadows, and no
one knoweth the time or manner thereof.
They were as hale in life's promises as I, and
were surrounded with accustomed concerns
and employments, while I was going out in
dangerous paths.

I joined the American Medical Association and attended three meetings; one at
St. Louis in 1854; in 1858 at Detroit; and
in 1867 at Cincinnati. These were national
gatherings where the great medical lumina-
ries assembled and many depending satelites
flitted around them in aweful and dangerous
homage. Therefore my office was to see
and hear; and, for the sake personal security,
to remain extremely quiet.

DECORATION DAY IN DECATUR IN 1869.

In May it became known that I had received the appointment of United States
Consul for the port of Vera Cruz, at the hand
of President Grant, and that I proposed to
sail to my post early in June. Decoration
Day was to be on Sunday, May 30th, and
on Thursday, June 27th, a committee from
the "Lodge of the Grand Army of the Republic," called on me and said they were

appointed to bear an invitation for me to be the orator of the day on the occasion of the celebration. I tried to plead my want of time, urgent business, want of oratorical faculties, others more capable, and many other valid excuses, but they replied that "they had no other names from which to choose, as the G. A. R. had given them but one name, and to that one they now applied, not wishing to take back to their Lodge 'no' for an answer." After some anxious hesitation I consented to act, and knowing that the audience would be a large one, and standing on damp ground , I determined to make the oration as short as possible, and was as follows:

THE ORATION.

Soldiers of the Grand Army of the Republic, Ladies and Gentlemen:

It is fitting that we should strew sweet flowers upon these graves. It is well to manifest what we feel towards our compatriot martyrs. And while we are willingly and earnestly thus engaged, it is but the counterpart of that which is transpiring this very hour in many, very many other hamlets and cities throughout the United States.

And although there are thousands of graves, or that which should be such, so situated that they cannot be dressed in evergreens, and fragrance, and beauty, as our sacred affections would clothe them could we gain their access, yet this memorial in the Decatur Greenwood Cemetery is in token of all soldiers who died in the recent rebellion, battling for the perpetuity of those hallowed principles of organic government which our forefathers, through much tribulation and blood, hath given us. By their blood our glorious country to-day stands out a salient and proud example; the hope and the hoped for, of all the down trodden and oppressed intelligences of the earth; the safe asylum in which their halcyon dreams of freedom, which dare not ask for interpretation under imperial crowns, stand redeemed.

Nor do these becoming ceremonies of the day, wherein our heart's libations are as the outpouring of the everflowing fountains, signify that a command should be given, in order that we, an ever greatful people, require that command to keep alive in our recollections the memory of our departed friends; nor that they are mimicry of sincerity and but the offspring of pageant pastime and vain display. But that command is given by a soldier's well organized head, in full sym-

pathy with every wound that bled, with every
eye that lost its lustre, in order that there
might be a concert of action throughout the
land, that mourners of departed friends may
know, that though the graves which contain
their idols are distant, or isolated, or lost
forever to human recognition, or are gathered under enduring marble bearing historic
inscriptions, yet it is, by actual presence or
in emblem, thus truly consecrated.

This quiet Sunday has been, by that order selected as a fitting occasion for us to
make another public demonstration in favor
of that unspeakable affection which all patriots feel for those whose fervor made them
a ready sacrifice for the perpetuity of this
glorious nation. We who now remain to
honor and respect those the patriot dead,
know little of the anguish which they endured. Men present may have suffered by
the side of those who sank; but they still
live to strike hands over the graves of their
fallen comrades, as they mingle their tears
with the fragrant flowers upon these mounds,
these monuments. They still live in glory
and honor, and long may they live to enjoy
the sweet fruits their valor won. But those
—our brothers "who wrapped the drapery
of the couch around them," and sank to
that eternal slumber, had more of mortal

wound, or dire disease, or less of earth to
hold them here than we. And to thus, and
and there, and then die were more than
ordinary death.

I have heard the dying patriot, in that
dread hour when heaven's heralds claimed
them as recruits in that far off army, beg but
to know, before they went, that the emblem
of their home-land—their heart's idolatry—
would be maintained. But they died, not
knowing that. They died, not surrounded
by the holy presence of domestic affections.
They died upon the tented fields, and laid
their uncoffined boddies upon the ensanguin-
ed soil, and often their bones were left to
bleach beneath a Southern sun. But to
thus die were after the order of the pleasing
sports of the Elysian gods in comparison to
that slow but certain march in hunger and
all the horrors which fiends could invent
by the 34,000 men at Andersonville; by the
21,000 men at Belle Isle and Libby prison;
by the 19,000 men at Selma, Charleston,
Mobile, and Montgomery; not naming the
victims of many other and minor places.—
An hundred thousand of the most shameless
and fiendish acts of animosity admonish us
to-day, as a grand army of selected veterans,
that this free country of ours, ransomed by
their blood, as a grand guard in the advance,

is now dispelling, by its examples, its blessings and its increasing intelligences, a deep clear lesson of humanity which, it is hoped, will forever hereafter prevent the re-enactment of such savage barbarity.

We have every reason, in our individual selfishness, to be thankful in the highest sense that we have lived to see this painful problem solved. We have also every reason to regret that these our fallen comrades could not have lived to behold the nation's prestige in this auspicious hour, And now, while we, in great humility, stand here, with wreaths and garlands to bedeck the tombs of departed heroes, on this consecrated ground, with these granite spires for testimonials; these files of human souls as witnesses, and God as our impartial judge, let us vow anew, in order that their blissful sleep may be more sweet, that this fair land in all its ransomed glory shall be maintained in honor, honesty and right; or we will join their incarnate legions through the same fiery road in which they took their flight from earth. That man should live upon the sea and claim no foothold upon the land to call his port, who, when his country is assailed by the destroyer, would flee its colors and ruthlessly and coweringly abandon its fate to the rapacious conduct of a conqueror. And if there ever

is a hallowed time when God doth give a
present victory, it is when aged parents
give up their sons to go upon the battle
field, armed with the firelocks their valiant
sires gave them; shielded by the prayers
their pious mothers offered, and reinforced
by the consciousness of right and the hope
of homes yet being continued free and happy, by the prestige of their young and man-
ly powers. This victory is an offering.—
This offering we can no more comprehend
and measure, than we can garner the full
effulgence of a noonday's sun. Its warming
beams surround us; its cheering radiance
enlivens us; its glorious halo dispells the
noxious vapors; its brilliancy and transpa-
rency are emblematical of that hoped for
cheerful home beyond the passover. But
when this offering becomes a sacrifice;
when these noble men are borne back upon
the shields of weeping comrades; then hew
the sarcophagi in the solid rocks and raise
the stately monuments on fruitful soils:

"Plant there some box or pine;
  Something which lives in winter
  And will be a verdant offering
  To their memory;"

for they have won the victory, and we now
enjoy, in the plenitude of God's mercy, the
full fruits of the sacrificial offering.

These spires admonish us that it is ours soon to join "the innumerable throng."— This City of the Dead in its unwritten charter proclaims to the living conscience, that, as a nation, as a people, and as individuals, we cannot prosper unless we are honest, just and true. And we can best dignify our conduct by those principles, and show our sincerity and friendship to those martyred heroes, by taking care of their remains; by providing for their widows and orphans, and by faithfully perpetuating the government for which they died. Our Soldier's Homes; our public munificent charities; our national and substantial Pension Bureau; our awards of place and power to the maimed and the offspring of the patriot slain; these testimonials; these flowers; these tears; this goodly attendance; all assert our hearts are right. Then let our acts obey the mandates of our hearts, and see, as a people and as individuals, that the posterity of those whom the God of battles has taken hence, shall never in true merit want. Let us take them into our enclosures and support them; take them into our homes and protect them; take them into our hearts and caress them; for these were their idols, their jewels; they are now their representatives, their remnants.

In conclusion, let me ask you here as often as you may, in concert and true harmony come, and bring your hearts full of compassion, your arms full of floral emblems, and renew your vows of fidelity and faith; pour consolation in substantial measure upon those who mourn departed friends; and may peace and a prosperous land be ours long to inhabit.

And now kind friends, I beg one word for parting. I sail in a very few days from this fair land, our noble country, our proud home, to make a temporary residence in the disorganized and dismembered nation of Mexico. In leaving Decatur and Illinois, I go from the house of "many mansions" in which I have been received and patronized beyond any expectation, and far beyond any merit of which I thought myself possessed. For all of this my heart will ever throb with grateful impulsations. My artless soul returns to you the compliment. God grant that you may all long live and be forever happy. Good bye, and God be with you.

APPOINTED CONSUL.

The preceeding paragraph prefaces this one and heralds the fact. The election to the Presidency of the United States of General Grant, gave me a friend and acquaintance in the White House who was ready to reward me for services rendered in his command while in the army. General Oglesby recommended me, and General Moore, our Congressman, then made the application, and my appointment and Commission were dated April 19. 1869. I left Decatur for Vera Cruz on the 7th of June, sailed from New Orleaens on the evening of the 9th, arrived in Havana on the 12th and remained there 12 days waiting for a steamer to go to my post of duty. During these 12 days in Havana, I had a fine opportunity to see the Spanish qualities of the volunteers then in full sway of the political situation, they just having deposed Captain Gen. Dulce. A letter I wrote to Mrs. Trowbridge from Havana while there and which was published in the Decatur papers, gives observations of things and persons as I saw them better then any recollection I may now retain.

I sailed from Havana in the "Royal Mail.

Steamer Tamar" Captain Herbert, a generous and intelligente Englishman, who was very anxious to discuss "Alabama Claims", and did it with great freedom and good nature. We arrived at Vera Cruz on the morning of the 28th day of June 1869, and I then learned that my predecessor Mr. E. H. Saulnier had died on the 16th, 12 days before my arrival, and had left the Consulate in the charge of his clerk. General Rosecrans was then Envoy Extraordinary and Minister Plenopotentiary at Mexico, although the Hon. Thomas H. Nelson had arrived as his successor but did not take possession of his office until the 1st. of July. My Commission from Washington was sent to the Legation at Mexico and on the 2. of July President Benito Juarez and his Secretary of State, Sebastian Lerdo de Tijada, now President of Mexico, sent to Mr. Nelson the official Exequatur, which Commission and Exequatur arrived in Vera Cruz July 11th, and I entered upon the official duties of the Consulate next day.

This happened to be a very important period. It was soon after the withdrawal of the Maximillian forces which had attempted to establish an Empire in Mexico, was also just at the close of our Great Rebellion, and a treaty between the U. S. and Mexico, to adjust claims of citizens of each republic respectively against the governments, was just then coming in force. These events therefor, required great care on the part of American officials in this country, to give full and efficient justice to their labors, and at the same time to do so in a manner accptable to both governments.

Mexico had cut cff all diplomatic and consular relations with France, England and Spain, and the U. S. Government had been asked to take charge of the French consular archives, and to transact her consular service through the U. S. Consulate at Vera Cruz. This was so done, and some dissatisfaction was felt over the transaction, although the Mexican government granted that this should be permitted.

There were also many disaffected secessionists, who would no longer live under the U. S. flag, then in the dependencies of this Consulate, and who were by no means courteous to the representatives of our government. Add to these circumstances the jealousy arroused by the many American citizens who were presenting fabulous claims against the Mexigan government, together with the fact that I was a new man just from the new authorities at Washington, which chiefest Authority had done more to

thrash out and disgrace the rebel element
here than any other man in all our nation,
I say, when these things come to be considered, it is not strange or untrue that I tho't
with good reason, that my arrival and first
labors were rather important and delicate.
I could not speak the language nor under-
stand many uncourteous sentences said concerning the "new consul." They were kind
enough not to interpret those rumors to me
and therefore I was unconscious of them
until a better state of affairs came, which improved public feeling I have tried to keep
increasing.

Soon after Mr. Nelson took charge of the
Legation he issued an order to all the consular officers in Mexico to report to him the
political status and resources of their respective districts. He doubtless had two objects
in this: viz. 1. To learn of our representatives the impressions of the country and what
it contained. and 2. to test the caliber of the
Consular Corps. I was a stranger in the land
and to the usual tone of diplomatic correspondence; but concluded that a straight forward expression of facts would meet his
wants, and therefore sailed in with the best
array of these which I could gather; and was
fortunate enough to win a complimentary
letter of thanks for my production. Soon

after this, a similar test came from the De-
artment of State, which, from my former
letter to Mr. Nelson, was more readily, and
to my mind, more satisfactorily answered.
On several occasions I have received complimentary acknowledgements for these reports from the State Department. This report to the Department was published in
Mexico, by orders from Washington to Mr.
Nelson. See Appendix, for this and several
other offiicial documents, which I believe is
all that is necessary to say of my official
transactions in the Consulate.

My family arrived in Vera Cruz via. New
York and Havana in the good Steam-Ship
"City of Mexico" Commanded dy Captain
John Deaken on the 29. day of October,
having encountered a terrible storm on the
Gulf of Mexico two days before landing in
Vera Cruz. For a discription of this voyage
see Appendix for a letter published in the
Decatur Magnet written by our eldest daughter, Ada. My family were not well pleased
with the social associations the new home
presented and returned to Decatur on the
20. day of June 1870.

Our fifth daughter

MAUDIE BEATRICE TROWBRIDGE

was born in Decatur November 28. 1870; a
bright and healthy little black eyed pet, of
whom the family was very proud and anxious to exhibit her beautiful little face to the
father, then over 2000, miles distant by the
most direct route. They embarked again for
Vera Cruz Feb. 2. 1871 via. New Orleans,
and arrived in the Mexican Steamer "Tabas-
co" Feb. 8. 1871. Little Maudie was but 9
weeks old at the commencement of this voyage and was very sick while on the Gulf,
with Conjestion of the brain. Mrs. T. treated her admirably, and when they came into port the precious babe gave me a
welcoming smile of such peculiar sweetness
that I shall never forget it. Ada was also
dangerously sick during this voyage, but
Mrs Trowbridge's clever medical skill restored her also to meet me in fine convalescence.

YELLOW FEVER.

On my arriving at Vera Cruz I learned
there were a few sporadic cases of Yellow
Fove here, and that we were in the midst
of the season which usually gave the largest

mortality from that much dreaded scourge.
1 had prior to reaching our more Southern
borders while in the army as surgeon, posted
myself by carefully reading all the standard
authorities on this disease; and while in
Havana en route for Vera Cruz, had seen
several cases. From these researches and
observations I became convinced that the
pathology of the affection was correct; and
if so, the treatment adopted to fill the indications of cure was wrong; and resolved to
pursue a different and independent course if
the disease should assail me. Seven days
after landing at Vera Cruz I was taken with
the malady. I knew not a soul in the city,
could not speak the language, and the prospect was not cheerful, to say the least of it,
as the ratio of deaths to the cases of attack,
was as one is to two.

The pathology of Yellow Fever is this,
in short: The specific virus causing the affection is not known. Yet its action on the
vital organs is very well marked. It assails
the mucous membranes of the stomach and
bowels, either directly or as a cause, producing destruction of them with rapidity, and
of course, deranging through sympathy and
reflex action, the kidneys, liver, brain and
general nervous system. To make myself
clear to the non-medical reader, I will illus-

trate.—If a blister be applied to the skin, a pouch of cuticle filled with serum is produced, because the inflammation detaches the scarf-skin, or cuticle, from the 2d layer (rete mucosum) which is dense, and will only allow the serum, or watery part of the blood, to strain through. The muscular layer of the skin lying just beneath the 2n layer bleeds red blood when the two first coats are broken. The intestinal tube has first a mucous membrane and next to this is the muscular coat. Now if anything causing inflammatory action of the mucous membranes occurs, they kreak down, and the muscular layer is at once exposed; and blood globules, or red blood, with serum, passes into the intestinal track.

Therefore, Yellow Fever, assailing these mucous membranes, breaks them down, when severe, and blood transudes into these organs, which soon becomes grumous or disintegrated, and is thrown off as "black vomit."

Hence it is clear, that whatever treatment is adopted which maintains the integrity of the mucous membranes intact, will prevent the escape of blood, as such, into the stomach and bowels, and prevent the possibility of the black vomit—a most fatal symptom.—

When attacked, I took a free purge of

Castor Oil, and followed it with frequent doses of Sulphite of Soda, Chlorate of Potassa, and such agents as are disinfectant, with the view to preserve the mucous membranes. These with hot foot-baths and fresh air constituted the treatment. I was sick but a short time, with no consequent sequel. Every member of my family had the disease in 1872 — 7 cases — and all recovered soon and perfectly, Maudie was but 6 months old when she took it, and Mrs. Trowbridge would have·been an extremely unpromising subject under the usual mode of treatment, being much the worst one of the family. She had gone to Illinos less than a year previously weighing 130 lbs, had spent the winter there, came back a mother of a young babe, was not aclimated, and weighed 180lbs. She was the last of the flock to take the disease, had been depressed with anxiety and care, and with all my prophylactics and best attentions, had several paroxysms of vomitsng a grumous dark coffee-round substance. She took a sinking spell and but for the immediate use of a direct diffusive stimulant, would have died without reaction in less than half an hour.

I have induced some medical men to use this mode of treatment, and with greatly improved result in every instance.

VICE CONSUL

I nominated my son Charlie for Vice Consul, Mr. Nelson endorsed the nomination and on the 28. day of March 1871, he was appointed by the Hon'. Secretary of State to that office, he being then only 15 years of age. In June 1872, I took my family to Illinois via. N. Y. leaving Charlie in charge of the Consulate, and was gone three months.

I left Mrs. Trowbridge, with our five girls in Decatur, and returned, arriving at Vera Cruz Sept. 11. finding all had gone well at the Consulate during my absence.

On the 25. day of Jan. 1873, I sent Charlie home to take care of the family during that terribly cold winter, he returning June 4. following.

MARRIAGE OF MR. FREDERICK M. PETERSEN TO MISS ADA B. TROWBRIDGE.

On the 4th day of May, 1873, our oldest daughter was married to Mr. Frederick M. Petersen, a thrifty whole-sale merchant of Vera Cruz, and a thoroughly refined and accomplished gentleman. Mr. Petersen soon after his marriage sailed for Europe to visit his relatives and partner in business, who live in Hamburg, and to purchase goods at the various manufacturing marts in Europe; and returning via. Decatur, he and his wife accompanied my family to Vera Cruz, arriving there Nov. 20. 1873, again via. N. Y. and Havana in the "City of Mexico," now commanded by the dashing Captain Sherwood.

My family had been gone this time over 17 months, and during the Spring of 1873, our little Maudie was violently assailed by Spotted Fever (Cerebro Spinal Aracnitis) and doubtless would have died had it not been for the able skill of Dr. Chenoweth.

On the 2d day of May 1874, my family and Mrs. Petersen visited the City of Mexico, enjoying a six days ramble with great relish. For a description of what we there saw, see Appendix.

The writing has caught up with transpiring events, and now, JULY FOURTH, 1874, I have

Only to add

A Dios.

U. S. Consulate
Vera Cruz.

THE END.

APPENDIX

TO THE

AUTOBIOGRAPHY

OF

S. T. TROWBRIDGE M. D.

CONTAINING

LETTERS, ADDRESSES, DISSERTATIONS, REPORTS,
ESSAYS AND MISCELLANEOUS
PRODUCTIONS
OF THE
AUTHOR,

APPENDIX.

FOURTH OF JULY 1858.

The following correspondence will sufficiently explain the Toast and speech that follows. — Ed.

DECATUR, JULY 6. 1858.

S. T. TROWBRIDGE, M. D.

DEAR SIR:–We, the undersigned citizens of Decatur, being deeply impressed with those sentiments of simple justice, which it pleased you, in reference to a toast given at the celebration in this place on the 5th inst., to pay to the worthy and generous philanthropists of revolutionary fame, who were and still are the illustrious representatives of the honored profession to which you belong; and feeling sensibly the public importance of those attributes into which you characterized your co-laborers in the great cause of human suffering, and fully believing that a knowledge of these sentiments will interest and enlighten the public mind on a subject of most vital importance, viz: that the members of the medical profession will not hold themselves responsible in character or name for the ruinous and fatal consequences which may attend the rightles efforts of the unlettered and illegitimate interlopers—we do therefore solicit from you for publication, a copy of the toast and your response thereto.

With the highest consideration of respect and esteem of your fellow citizens,

J. S POST.	ANSEL TUPPER.
R. IRWIN.	G. W. VERMILLION.
G. LEFORGEE.	A. A. STAFFORD.
A. D. RISDON.	J. IMBODEN.
CHAS. C. POST.	C. R. WHEELER.
W. J. CHENOWETH.	I. B. CURTIS.
S, Y. BALDWIN, and others.	

DECATUR, JULY 9th, 1858.

GENTLEMEN:—Yours of the 6th inst, is before me. You have my thanks extended to you at this my earliest opportunity, for the honor conferred by requesting a copy of my response on the 5th, at our celebration, in answer to the call of Mr. Ansel Tupper's toast to "The Doctors." And now at your solicitation, which has been so courteously bestowed, I herewith enclose a copy nearly as can be, of the remarks I made on that occasion and pass them into your hands to do with as you see proper.

With many sensations of gratitude I remain gentlemen, your most humble and obedient servant.

S. T. TROWBRIDGE.

J. S. POST,
R. IRWIN,
A. TUPPER,
 and others.

[THE TOAST.]

The Doctors.

Highest in the ranks of professional men are the members of the Medical Faculty. May the anatomical skill of that assiduous class supplant discovered errors by lessons of science drawn from the bones of Quacks.

A. TUPPER.

APPENDIX.

LADIES AND GENTLEMEN:—In answering to a sentiment so flattering to the members of the medical profession, I feel that the proffered honor transcends my capabilities, and yet I have the weakness to make a trial. We acknowledge the compliment, so liberally bestowed by an accomplished member of a rival profession, which is paid in the toast; and to the prayer of which, that "may the anatomical skill of that assiduous class supplant discovered errors by lessons of science drawn from the bones of Quacks" I can most heartily say Amen! And now turning this toast and sentiment to the fitness of this day, which is truly one of glory—a type and symbol of all those days of struggle and self-sacrifice for the institutions which constitute our creed of republicanism, I am happy to say that round those council fires which our Fathers kindled, many prominent members of the Medical Profession clustered and afforded an efficient corps of operatives in those days, which truly tried the souls of men. Allow me here to halt and call some names. Benjamin Rush, was a signer of the Declaration of Independence and one of Philadelphia's finest Doctors. Gen. Joseph Warren, who, by his eloquence and example contributed so largely to arouse his townsmen to resist the aggression of England, and who at the battle of Bunker Hill, led on the repeated charges until the Peace Angel from the Purer Land proclaimed his victory won, and called his councils to the courts of Heaven, was a Doctor; and his younger brother, Dr. John Warren, volunteered as a

private soldier, which is proof positive that he
was impelled by patriotism alone to take the
noble step. In being called upon then, this
day, to answer to a sentiment, which shall em-
brace that of my profession, it is expected I
suppose, that this opportunity is given for me
to elucidate the peculiar manner in which medical men fight their battles and gain their golry.
While ambition in her military garb stands forth
under the stimulus of passion and braves the
booming blasts of its adversary and sinks or
swims in the crimson of its carnage to the goal of
glory, has always played the part of the destroyer;
"it is ours with a higher civilization — a more
holy heroism — which has ever saught to save.

Our battles are fought in the lazar house, the
hospital and the plague stricken districts, where
the courage of the warrior under the promptings
of passion or the greed of applause can hardly be
compared to the noble intrepidity of the surgeon
who gleans in the ruthless and red-handed reaper's
path the leavings of the battle, and still less with
the hero of the hospital who encounters the grim
antagonist in the dread of silence and the gloom
of groans and pestilence. Imagination can hardly
embody an instance of human courage and virtue
more sublime and unearthly than that of the physician who, in the midnight of a plague stricken
city, threads the fœtid solitudes of its alleys and
entering the doomed hovel of the wretched, ministers to the perishing, while only pestilence and
misery, death and God are witnesses"

I need not leave this ground to grasp the hand
of those who claim no laurel, those whose philanthropic labors in sacred scenes like these, have

been unmarked save by the Eye that never slumbers and remembered only by Him who alone will reward.

One feature more and I am done. When epidemics scourge the land and lives are sacrificed simply by remaining in the infected district; as for instance it was at Norfolk, Virginia, three years ago, where forty graves are this day watered by the tears of a greatful people and only ten remained to do battle with one of the most terrific affections, when not one of that genera recognised as a "regular physician" has been found to abandon his perilous post, but stood, with all the powers he had on earth, his life included, to ransom from the couch and bier the many wending thitherward; when I force upon your recollections these reflections, then I can say that these are the standards by which we wish to be measured and such the men to "draw the lessons of science from the bones of Quacks."

--------- *** ---------

An incident of the celebration. MR. N. W. TUPPER was the orator of the day, and during the delivery of his oration, dislocated his shoulder joint. I was marshal of the occasion, and was sitting on the stand, and seeing the painfub situation of Mr. Tupper, immediately placed him supine upon the floor and readily reduced the dislocation. The speaker on rising asked what he was saying when the accident occured, and being told by the chaplain, the Rev. D. P. BUNN, at once took up the thread of his discourse, saying "this specimen of grund and lofty tumbling was merely exhibited by way of parenthesis."

APPENDIX.

An Adventure In New York City.

[From The Decatur Magnet, September 22. 1859.]

One of our eminent physicians paid New York city a visit a few weeks since; and, from the accounts we have heard, he came within an ace of losing his life. It appears that, when nearing the city, after night, he became slightly acquainted with a gentleman in the cars, who sat upon the same seat with him and from whom he gained the right direction from the landing of the ferry boat to the Merchant's Hotel, on Courtland St, which was near by. The doctor, feeling tired after so long a trip in the cars, concluded he would walk to the hotel. But he had not proceeded far when he was hailed by dozens of runners from different houses in the city. The doctor told them he preferred walking, as the distance to the Merchant's was not very great,

"The Merchant's—Merchant's! come along, come along with me, and I will take you there," said a sharp looking fellow, "I am runner for that house," The doctor, without further ceremony, gave the 'runner' his valise, and followed closely behind him. After a while, the parties turned a corner, and the doctor observed to his companion, that, from what he had learned of a gentleman in the cars, the Merchant's Hotel was on the street where the boat landed. He was told that it was a mistake, and that he would soon reach his desired destination. After turning two or three corners and falling in with another runner, or robber, they arrived at a hotel. The doctor stepped into the office, and was requested by the landlord to register his name.

"If this is the Merchant's Hotel, I will

register my name, but I believe I have been deceived by your runner."

"You are all right—this is the Merchant's—register your name," said the landlord.

The doctor, still entertaining doubts, began to question 'mine host' again; and was told that he was not in the Merchant's, but one equally as good. He did not think so. He told the landlord he would not register his name, but would go to the Merchant's at once.

"Well, sir," said the landlord, in a passion, "you must pay your bill here before you leave."

"I owe you no bill" replied the doctor, somewhat irritated by such ungentlemanly treatment.

"You do, sir! I have to pay my runners one dollar apiece for customers. Pay me a dollar and a half, or I'll blow your brains out!" exclaimed the landlord frothing with anger, and at the same time flourishing a revolver before the astonished gaze of our western Esculapius.

The doctors feelings and position at this crisis can be better imagined than described. There stood his adversary in a threatning attitude, with pistol drawn, and apparently eager to engage in mortal combat; while he, friendless and defenceless, must, as he thought, stand a target for a villain to shoot at. But he remained perfectly calm. In a moment a happy thought seized him. Looking straight into his antagonist's face, with a firm and determined air, he thrust his hand into a side pocket in his coat, and said, almost without moving a muscle, "Sir I owe you nothing. You have deceived me, and brought me here against my will. Now put away that pistol

or I will blow your brains out?" And the landlord actually did as commanded, and the doctor
was permitted to go in peace. After a few moments' travel he found the Merchant's Hotel;
and, with a trembling hand he registered his
name. This was his first visit to Gotham.

☞ NOTE. The foregoing is in the main
correct; save that the said doctor told no one
to what hotel he was going. And the runner was
sitting on the rear steps of the Merchant's Hotel
omnibus, and sang out to the doctor, as he passed
it, "Merchant's Hotel Sir? Thereby deceiving
the doctor as to the runner's true intentions and
place of employment.

APPENDIX.

The Effect of Wearing Mourning, upon the Mourner.

A Thesis Read to the Macon County Medical Society, at the Regular Meeting held at Decatur, April 3. 1860, by S. T. Trowbridge.

Published in Accordance with a Resolution of said Society.

Mr. President and Fellows: — It is not the purpose of the writer to review the history of the times and fashions which gave origin to the present custom of wearing mourning apparel for those of our friends and relatives who have passed beyond the realm of time; but dispassionately and without the influence of prejudice to give, according to the significance of the heading, the evil effect of wearing mourning weeds for the dead upon the remaining mourner.

It is objectionable for four reasons; viz:

1. Because it does not lesson our afflictions.

2. Because of its non universality.

3. Because mourning habiliments are mere things of fashion, when excuse is rendered to employ them, and as such, often intesifying to danger, emotions otherwise supportable.

4. Because when sober second thought is brought to bear upon the subject, nothing but ridicule and contempt can be entertained for the custom.

The first proposition is self-evident from the fact, that, although we comply with a fashion and thereby evince our respect for the departed in this way; the mind of the truly distressed considers not in what condition the persons of the surviving being caressed in the partial lap of fortune. But, as a consolation to all this, "we are taught that the grave regards not man for his worldly wealth or honor."

In regard to the third objection, that mourning habiliments are mere things of fashion when excuse is rendered to employ them, and as such, often intensifying to danger, emotions otherwise supportable, it is thought that this will be acceded to when a few illustrations are presented. That this is a mere fashion no one will deny even without reflection. And as before said, by constantly recurring to our losses or the mementoes which point to them, we foster and nourish a dissipation, the effect of which, on delicate and sensitive constitutions, but too often transcends the best directed efforts of scientific medical aid. Then considering the custom in this light and viewing the appalling consequences which sometimes result from it, the question arises to every candid mind as to whether this is not another form of what we might consistantly call sentimental suicide. If the custom does not have this effect or a tendency to it, then it has none whatever, and according to our fourth proposition or objection which we gave you, is only entitled to our silent contempt and untold ridicule. But before discussing our last objection. I desire to draw upon your imaginations for the following hypothetical case and see if it is over wrought. We will assume that Mr. A. is the husband of a loving, delicate and dyspeptie wife, the father of a family of senitive young daughters; himself a consumptive by hereditary desent, who has just paid the debt of nature and left the rough world

to his affectionate widow and her tender children.
Now dress them in deep crape and teach them,
as this will, to yield to the depressing influences;
let the mother's eyes behold her beautiful orphans
sit pensive and despondant in their draped apparel; let to-morrow see them thus arrayed again,
and again the anguish of yesterday is theirs to
sustain. I will not ask professional minds alone
to follow me in the rehearsal of this dreary and
desolate case further, in order to conclude that
damages, almost beyond the reach of remedies,
will be the sad and inevitable effect of the foolish
fashion. Where is the daughter in whose bosom
heaves the grateful impulsations of maternal love
that can see the heavy weight, kept heavy ad
infinitum, by mourning memorialized, and still
enjoy either health or even life itself? Then behold the sympathetic mother return sadness for
sadness increasingly until Dyspepsia, Scrofula
and Consumption shall fasten their remorseless
fangs deep in their vital fountains and fresh cause
for weeping will soon be added to the dismal
scene. But as an offset to all this we have the
simple fact to state, which is, that the fashion is
only adopted by a part of the community, while
the more contemplative reject it altogether.

We cannot express our disapprobation as my
fourth objection might lead one to suppos to the
usage, at the time and to the persons who are
freshly applying the dark regalia; but we can entertain our own thoughts, nor can we well re-
strain them, and we have thought it profitable
to expose the demerits and unhealthy influences
arising from it, to this society. With me the language of weeds is often after this wise. When I

see a tall white hat with a broad crape band upon
it it says to me—"here is my playcard of distress.
see how bad I feel how melancholy give me
your pity and sympathy and watch me while I
weep —I cannot say that they who adopt the
fashion are moved by such impressions—surely I
hope not. But it would be wrong for any one, to
place himself in such society, for verily, that is
not the true sensations nor manner of bearing
our misfortunes. Let it not be understood, by
the foregoing, that we are putting in our protes-
tations against the pageantry sometimes sought
to be made by those bereaved of their relatives
at the time of burial, for this serves as relief at
the time most needed and tends to decoy the
mind from the subject of its sorrow. But to continue this display from day to day and from year
to year; even in the sense of the subject of these
objections; is as inappropriate as it would be to
continue the rehearsal of the obsequies and funeral services for as long a time. Nor do I ask you
to forget those who are forever gone; but I would,
if it were pertinent to my subject, call upon you
to cherish their memory and venerate them, for
from the grave their many virtues shine; but I
will ask you to abstain from putting their memory as a cloak upon the surface—from wearing it
as a garment until the brittle tissues fade from
first to second and all the subsequent gradations
of mourning that fashion mongers may invent.
The tricksters in the trade would seek to have
one born in a fashionable stream of time; live
in fashionable leading-strings, die according to
their dictum and after that to have our mourners
follow the visions of their chimerical whims for

from one to five years with strict observance. Has not the civilization of this progressive nineteenth century one sacred retreat, one holy place of refuge; even this one last lonely relief from the speculating influence of ignoble fashion? If the requirements of this age are such that we must have the "a la mode," then let it be of the chamelion hue—as others are—let us turn white occasionally; for certainly that color can be advocated as successfully as any other class. If we adopt these ordinances in order that we may show respect for the dead, and at the same time believe that the departed soul is with its God, then why not wash our garments of all stains and doff the drooping crape for robes such as angels wear? Surely our present color is typical of the fear which is within us.

Now, in conclusion, for a people who read the reverent book of God, and are thereby blessed with enlightened christian civilization and learn from that sacred oracle of the white robes the seraphs, angels and Savior wore after this world's transitory death, and the proofs we have of the immortality of the soul, to adopt the present mode of fashionable mourning transcends contemplative sober thought and stagnates common sense.

PLACED UNDER THE PLATES OF EACH
MEMBER OF MY FAMILY, ON THEIR RETURN
FROM LONG VOYAGES AND AN ABSENCE.
OF 18 MONTHS.

THE REUNION.

Let us thank the RULING PROVIDENCES.
for the plenitude of our unbounded pleasures in
being permitted to break bread with all the
dear ones of our harmonious household assembled
in good health, after a separation of 531 days.
The bliss of this hour is too sacred to be marred
by giving any details of this last past year and
a half; even the more pleasart passages are as
expended mythes when compared with the full
flowing fountains of contentment we feel after
those eight long voyages over land and sea have
been successfully made, the sum of whose distances amounts to 45,000 miles or more, and calls
for our gratitude to GOD for again giving these
happy healthful faces to commune together with
hearts in harmonious concord with each other
and all the everlasting past, and hopes compass-
ing the broadest sublunary beneficences, even exceeding these, and far reaching to that glorious
rest with those who have gone beyond the crude
currents of time, and who minister providences
under the guidance of God to us their earthly
charges.

I pray that all our lives may long be spared
for earth's consistant walks in health, prosperity
and happiness.

Your Affectionate Husband and Father,

E. T. TROWBRIDGE.

Vera Cruz, November 30. 1873.

LECTURE,

BY S. T. TROWBRIDGE, M. D. BEFORE THE LADIES, LITERARY LIBRARY ASSOCIATION, FEBRUARY 27. 1868.

AS MEDICAL MEN WHAT WILL MAKE US BETTER?

No person can conscientiously belong to a profession, trade or occupation without having the desire largely developed that the same should not only be respectable, but that its march of onward progress shall be at least as rapid and correct, as the pursuits of others which pass under his observation.

Being identified with the Medical profession, and called upon to speak aloud to my fellow-citizens upon some subject, I have, of course, an inclination to do so upon a topic, the bearing of which is common to us both. Hence when the compliment came to me from the Ladies' Library Association, asking that I give a public address for their benefit, the flattering unction was too sweet for me to refuse; and my hopes so sanguine, and heart so ardent for the success of the effort these ladies are putting forth, that I am here to–night to say a word for them.

One year ago my colleague and predecessor in in the office of President of the Macon County Medical Society met you, or a small number of you, and told you that it was the duty of the retir-ing President to deliver a public address upon some medico-popular subject, and in compliance with that duty, and the invitation of the L. L. A. I have selected, as the subject of remark, the foregoing inquiry: "As Medical men what will make us better?" I consider this a fitting theme for thought; one in which you, as the recipients of our skill, and we, the "hewers of wood" in this case, are equally concerned; for, as is our ability and knowledge of how life may be prolonged, and pain and anguish lessened, so will be those ends attained.

You, or those who take your places represented in our common society, must ere long take up that last, lone, sad march to the gloomy gates of time, and, passing them, leave mortality behind. But before you go, those hours of anguish will ask for aid. — Help us, kind friends, to give it.

That which elevates us, saves you. Could I print in golden letters a sentence, and hang it on the heavens that the precept should become exemplified, and its beneficent offices measured again in ten-fold blessings, it would be that one, coupled with the Biblical admonition, added to Medicine, "Do unto others as thou wouldst that they should do unto thee."

In the inquiry as to what will make us better, I can point to several things which, if effected, would work radical changes in the line of progress. I will call your attention to a few things which, if accomplished, would show good fruit.

Among these, the support that

LAW AND LEGISLATION

May give to medicine, has ever been a subject to which partizans have attached themselves, and

for and against which the divided mind of the
medical profession has for years been disputing.
While in all other pursuits and professions save
this the law is known to wield protecting power,
acknowledged to be indispensable to their perpetuity and welfare, yet here, true to the heralds of
missunderstanding, is left a beneficent profession
to stand alone, or fall to the ignominious disgrace
of an outlaw. The same persons who deprecate
the passage of statutory enactments for us, encourage them in all other departments of life's
employments. Now why it is that people who
live under the blessings of protecting regulations,
and appreciate their wholesome qualities, among
which may be found the first great law of nature
—self-preservation—should turn their backs upon
one of its most essential codes, is beyond my frail
comprehension. This has been done in several
instances through our law-makers in our State
Legislature, in refusing the passage of bills, prepared to their hands, to protect you against the
destructive practice of permitting incompetent
pretenders to administer medicine under circumstances which are attended with results and consequences mournfully appaling. It goes largely to
prove that reproachful epithet applied to mankind
is founded in fact, which asserts that men when
ungoverned and without the restraints of law are
incompetent to take care of themselves! Do not
start with horror at this expression, for it was
made by one of more brains and experience
than your humble speaker, and after a lifetime
spent in a field fruitful for such observations.
If men without compulsory restraints do not
take care of themselves when enjoying an im-
munity from disease; and if it is conceded also

that when the days of distress do come that their ability is less for this accomplishment, then is it humanity to withhold the helping hand? Is it a manifestation of moral courage to so scourge the subdued? Or is it another exemplification of that penetrating judgement which has discovered, as did one of our sage Senators from Chicago and the Chairman of the committee on Education last winter at Springfield, when speaking on this point; said, that "our mothers know more of medicine than the authors even of your books?"

It is true that medicine has ever been supported without the aid of law; and it pays the profession a graceful compliment to say that it has thus far maintained a growing existence—and this day, without legal assistance, possesses a more worthy confidence among cultivated minds, than at any time since the world began. This fact has headed a party who think, or pretend to, that had medicine been patronized by law and been protected as it is asked for by those who advocate the legislaion for it, that it would have rendered lethargic and dormant those very hands which now are ever active contributors to her present proud position. Is it compulsion and poverty that develops the talents and genius of Mott, and Mussey, and Brainard, and Holmes, and Brown-Siquard, and Bigelow, and Davis, and Gross, and a thousand others of our own dear country, who are wealthy, and who have stood and many of them are still standing at the head of their profession; guarding, from their exalted watch-towers all the avenues of intelligence and learning with diligent and jealous eyes, that they may lead on to continued advancement and commendable excellence? If some of the obstacles which have

hindered and impeded their progress heretofore
be removed, and a smooth road presented for their
advance, would these men lie down in lazy lethargy
and exclaim: "My great ambition is satisfied and
all my ends obtained?" No! they are not of the
class of men who seek the society of Mr Micaw-
ber and patiently wait for "something to turn up,"
as the zeal manifested in medicine to-day will
plainly show. But it is not the forced efforts which
pinching want crowds upon people who are compelled to labor which yield those abundant and
brilliant results that typify the genius of the most
complete success It is the love of the specific
labor of their election in such channels which
have produced them. As well might you say
that Farada would not have been a genius and
an energetic man had he been rich; that he would
have been heedless to all progressve investigations
in the sciences, and profligated his precious time
and talents at the shrine of flippant pleasure. But
no; his hours of pleasure were those in which
genius revelled with a romantic determination to
pioneer where no man had ever gone before; and
although poor, yet did he overcome the obstacles
which poverty presented, and launched into the
dogmatical speculations of electricity, to discover
and perfect to its present growth the doctrine of
Induction. Was it force-put poverty that ripened
the genius of Robert Burnes? Would not his
poems have presented even more of the essence
of soul had he had less of the "wormwood and of
the gall" mixed with his daily duties? Were
Byron and Moore less in their weight of talent
because surrounded by the creature comforts of
life? Is it not a fact that he who is stamped with

the golden star of genius will exercise his qualities and put forth the antlers of his talents just in consonance with his temporary surrounding circumstances. And wealth may add or subtract and poverty may do the same, and so with associations in society which are surrounding circumstances. But you may as well try to teach Dr, Johns or Mr. J. J. Jones that their fine blooded calves, if buffeted and starved and left unhoused in inclement weather, will soonest and best display their cast and finely proportioned qualities, as to say to me that genius can receive no aid, no assistance, or that the medical profession is best off by permitting any person to practice its calling who may wish, even though they may not know the most rudimentary outline of what is necessary in order to deal with the lives of their patrons understandingly.

I asked our last Legislature the passage of a law prohibiting any person from practicing medicine, surgery and the specialties in the state of Illinois unless the same should possess a diploma given to them for their own qualifications in the several departments of medicine from some chartered school of medicine. Mind you, I was not sectarian in this. I did not ask that it should be "regular," but any chartered medical college, which would admit to practice all kinds of doctors—Hydropaths, Homœopaths, Eclectics Botanics, &c., &c., if they should chance to emanate from any school supported by a charter of their kind or quality. In case a person desiring to practice medicine or any of its branches as specialties, and not possessing a diploma as above required, the "bill" provided for a board of medical examiners, whose duty it would be to examine into the practicle qualifications of each applicant, and if competent, to license all such as were found worthy.

It is known that there are hundreds who do not possess a diploma and are to-day practicing medicine not only here, but in many other States. Some of these are good men and well qualified, and of course this board will recognize and license them as such. But there are others on whom the mark of Cain is printed! Painted in the red blood of innocence by the vile hand of delusion! Stained on the young brow of infancy! Ingrained in the wrinkles and grey hairs of old age, and blended with the crooked wisdom which murders middle life! And by their works shall ye know them.

As a sample of their quality of competence, I will exhibit some specimens of medical preparations, and relate some cases in which the same were applied.

This vial contains a compound of equal quantities of Sweet Spirits of Nitre and Tincture of Veratrium Viride, which was ordered to be given to a citizen of Macon County, by a man practicing medicine in his neighborhood, in teaspoonfull doses every two hours. An ordinary teaspoon holds about 100 drops of such a fluid, which would be about 50 drops of the tincture of veratrium viride every two hours; or, ten average doses for an adult at once, of a most energetic and dangerous medicnie. Of course the patient was soon thought to be sick enough to send for other help and obtained it with no large margin to save life. This patient's disease at this time was simple remittant fever and quackery, with symptoms of the latter most alarming. I ask in the name of all common sense and honest humanity, would this man have given such destuctive doses if he had been properly schooled? Is there a Chartered Medical College of any kind in the whole United States which would not have given their students a better knowledge of these dangerous though valuable medicines than this? Dare they hazzard their reputation as teachers by graduating such talents to represent them? Is it at all probable that such a standard of knowledge could procure license to practice medicine from any board of examiners any Governor would appoint or any Senate of the State of Illinois would confirm? And would it not have been infinitely better had our patient been let entirely alone and to have trusted to nature's constitutional ability to throw off a disease not dificult to dispose of rather than to receive at the hand of brazen ignoranc such criminal treatment? That same conscientious gentleman still practces his "calling" in Macon County! He has no license to practice; is a graduate of no medical college; he belongs to no medical society! And hence you may know them.

This specimen is half ounce of red precipitate to the ounce of water to be taken in teaspoon full doses every three hours after thoroughly shaking. He took three portions and then sent for other help to cure his mouth, which was the worst sallivated one I ever saw. He was a quick witted Fenian; and said to me, as I querried him concerning his case, "red medicine will kill the devil; and doctor won't you plase give me white?" His Majesty having a fair chance to be slain with his case, and indications permitting, I gave white medicine as he wanted, to his tedious and painful recovery. I cannot say whether this Irishman had in his allusion to color, any political "war upon the races," but if so the resulting symbol was in favor of the Anglo-Saxon.

We might multiply infinitely such cases in all departments of medicine, and show you that good sharp-eyed intelligence is constantly being imposed upon by such men. Locality, convenience, interest, friendship, affiliation with beneficiary societies, associations with churches, or, what is as common cause as any, some white-washed medical sophistry flippantly pronounced, will frequently induce the trial of a prescription in the hope that it will do just as well as to go to the trouble of getting reputable and tried skill, which may be comparatively inaccessible. This step once taken in a case is, for obvious reasons, never abandoned, as a rule, in time to save regrets. Then, if this be so, there are logical reasonings to be deduced from it in favor of legislating as to the qualifications of those who are permitted to practice in the Medical Sciences. I have observed within the past year that quite a number of cases have presented themselves, wherein the life of the patient has been in peril, because of practices similar to these rehersed, and I presume that others of this society have as frequently met them. I am safe in saying there have been at least 6 such cases passed my knowledge, and we have over twenty members of this society wherefore, if each has had the half dozen cases, will reach the aggregate number of 120, all coming within the range of Macon County for the current year. Now, if an epidemic should have swept over this fair county, attacking 120 of its citizens, and dangerously threatening their lives and inflicting pain and lasting lameness upon them, then would there have gone up from the pulpit, the press, and the people, a wail for any sanitary regulation which would give promise of safety from its pestilent touch.

The two cases which it was my pleasure to select, recovered; but there are others for whom the pall-bearers have had to exercise their mournful mission to bear their precious burthens hence, for the cold clods to cover the errors of delusion. The Medical Profession is charged with all these cases, and it is such dangerous customs we desire to stop; and legislation on this point, in our humble judgement, will arrest them and create an exodus from our State of those obnoxious elements, and hence largly contribute to make us better in appearance and in fact.

The medical man is not to be read in professinal character with the same facility and certainty of accurate appreciation as any member of the other learned professions. There are many reasons why this is so. The minister of Theology in his pulpit labors to make plain to his auditory the intricacies of his text—stands with all his ability and eloquence to the elucidation of the doctrine he desires to establish, and all can easily see and appreciate his talents and award to him his true grade of merit.

Better still with the profession of Law. The lawyer engages in the advocacy of one interest, a plaintiff for instance, while his competitor is pitted against him in the interest of the adversary or defendant, and each sets forth the strength there is in their cause just as are their ability to do so. All can judge intelligibly of their comparative merit, and no field of intellectual labor opens so fair a prospect to genius and toil as this, for their efforts are always a measure of arms with a Judge of their own profession for an umpire. Theology and Medicine have to deal with the immutable laws of God, while on the other hand the lawyer has only to comprehend and labor in the intricacies of those laws of his own creation. Theology and Law are their own advocates; while the tongue of Medicine is mute. How perfectly easy then with these professional peculiarities to see the true merit of personal skill to which these two branches of letters give so many flattering examples. And how absolutely dissimilar are the habits and necessities of the Medical Profession from either of the foregoing? The mode of being educated; their anatomical studies, and the popular prejudices against any one who prosecutes them; the necessary secrecy and reticence concerning the same, and still in addition, the fact that we have no auditory before whom to appear for a discourse or explanation, which may set forth facts indicative of the amount of medical knowledge which may be possessed; the individual responsibility which only in consultations can be divided; the peculiarly impressive nature of that; responsibilitthe difference of being correctly understood by an audience or Jury; the clouded criticisms which come in lieu of this understanding when the motives of Medical men are under inspection, all go to indicate how easy the assent to excellence with Theology and Law, while for us how rough the road! If He who on the Mount proclaimed to fallen man His promises of future peace in Purity had added one more expression, and said, 'Blessed are they who on earth are misunderstood and maliciously misrepresented, for they shall some day receive other pay than epithets of ingratitude,' then would the forlorn and disconsolate worthies in Medicine hang like the anchor of hope on the promise and praise the ineffable prospect "beyoned where Styx's turbid waters roll," for never on this side is it expected that those prospects will ever be realized by the votaries of medicine.

To ask that a law be passed for the protection of medicine, is to ask for additional securities to be thrown around the precious life of every human being of our flourishing State; and to persistently refuse such aid is to pall the ardor and zeal of a class of men whose labors have contributed more to the true stock of knowledge throughout the dominion of letters, arts and sciences than any other one, and to endanger and jeopardize the fairest promise and most flattering prospect of a continuance of these same important results of zealous labor. The loud language of humanity calls out for its passage. The advancement and perfection of all the arms and branches

of knowledge are equally interested that a support be given, and cultivation by all collateral
avenues be exercised. We will urge nothing
farther for the maintenance of our medical standing by way of a general law if this one be granted; but will fervently ask that a

SPECIAL LAW BE PASSED LEGALIZING DISSECTIONS.

But here let us tread with commendable caution. This law when framed must meet only the
end engaged. No man who is not a cannibal
can desire a general law passed granting the
privileges of dissections to any, and all persons,
nor that all persons should be exposed to the
liability of being dissected after death. Since
man's earliest commencement of the march of time
has the deep repulsive prejudice existed against
the practical study of Anatomy. The "Form
Divine" has, since Adam's household first sang
in the fresh morning of creation, been held in
such holy reverance that even the dead remnants
of mortality must be embalmed and entombed,
and thus put to rest, bedewed with the consecrated tears which true affection distills, and permitted to moulder and subside into the results of
earth's mutations, rather than that the same
inanimate clay should be touched by the prying
blades of investigation.

No matter how much human suffering might
have been averted, yet for centuries the laws of
almost all the nations stood forth to hold its
manacles and flaming faggots over those who
might attempt to learn, from ocular observation,
the mysteries of this vitalized machine.

Men were mercilessly murdered to satiate the thirst which Nero had for blood; the brutal monster gave his fulsome orders to draw and quarter the corpses to gratify the same base and horrible spirit; but the man who would dare to ask this "tabernacle of the soul" one solitary question that might mitigate the maladies we mortals inherit was warned by the "stake and pile" that to trespass thus and there were tortures for the law. Are all the Neros dead and every Roman inconsistany obliterated? I only wish they were. History gives no details of any dissections, permitted or ordered, for the cultivation of surgical science. And in this century popular prejudices are still more mighty and menacing than the mandates of the statutes; medical men have been mobbed and murdered for the alleged attempt to carry on the practical study of anatomy; medical colleges have been leveled with the surface of the earth because dissections were tolerated and taught within their walls. Suffering humanity and the administrations of those who would relieve from the same, have one common interest that these prejudices be removed and a healthy standard, supported by law, be instituted in its place.

The law that will not now allow of these dissections, and popular prejudices, which are still more obnoxious to them, demand, in monied consideration, that the practice of the physician shall be so governed, by competent skill, as to be beyond the reach of malicious prosecutions for malpractice.— There is for this a better day now rising for the future; and as a symptom of its advent we will call your attention to the fact that those times and nations which gave the strongest oppositions to the act of obtaining knowledge by the study of practical anatomy, were the "Dark Ages" when men went forth to battle, scorning the overtures of surgical assistance. And those times and nations which fostered these studies most, were those of the highest civilization and the most extensive letters. And these two concomitants (civilization and letters) which are now so majestically heaving their heads above the horizon, and presenting to the bewildered gaze of the admiring multitudes, new fields for thought, new eyes for observation, when more can be accomplished in a day, than in years past could be brought about in a month; whose centenarian epoc has lengthened the days of a generation fifteen years or fifty per centum, over what it was a hundred years ago.

This day begins to demand that medical men shall know of what the human frame is made, and all that may be known by a minute and diligent study of all the long array of organizations of the human system.

No man, during our late war, could obtain, in this State, a position as surgeon or assistant surgeon, unless his personal qualifications showed him to be in possession of all the essential outlines and minutiæ of the anatomical man. Common sense demanded that this should be so. The scalding tears of praying mothers at home, dried up one-half their acrimony when this was known, and valor took a bolder stand, backed, as it were, by surgical competence.

And now the pertinent question comes,

How did you gain your knowledge? and the impertinent and humiliating answer: We stole our subjects to dissect. For there are no persons in our State privileged to get them within the limits of the State, unless they steal them, save those who sell themselves prior to being hanged. It requires, to make it legal, yet, in this broad blaze of civilization and intelligence, the sale which one may make of himself before a medical man can publicly dissect a subject. Our medical colleges steal all their subjects either directly or otherwise, by purchasing of some one who does; and this, of course, from compulsion.

A physician and surgeon is expected, by the community, to be a moral and an upright man. The public at large demand that he shall be well informed in all the channels of professional knowledge. The law gives heavy damages for malpractice. And yet you, by refusing him legalized dissecting privileges, compel him to be an ignorant pretender and an absolute know-nothing; or, if accomplished and skilled, he must be so by first becoming an out-law and a thief. The people and the law demand the knowledge; the same implacable powers still unrelentingly persist in keeping the doors closed by which that knowledge may be obtained. Now, what counter blasts of hot and cold are here! Let me give you a practical example; An Assemblyman has a ruptured artery in the arm-pit; calls upon a surgeon to treat him; the surgeon finds it necessary to tie the artery between the bursted place and the heart, which would prevent the blood from running into the diseased or bursted vessel. A knowledge of anatomy would teach him exactly where the artery ran and where other important organs were situated. The life of the patient depends upon the skill of the operator, and his skill depends mainly upon his knowledge of those organs, and his knowledge is only to be obtained by continued and careful dissections. The assembly man votes down the law granting to any one the right to dissect, and then either employs a surgeon who has directly or indirectly stolen his information, if he be competent to treat his case successfully, or dies, as he must, under the care of one who is willing to stop where law and society want he should — in which case the physician (for he could not be a surgeon then) is liable to be sued for his incompetence and made to pay heavy penalties for doing just as consistance with the law and the assembly man's vote would dictate, was all that should have beed done. Now, please look on both sides of this question and see if there is not something rotten in this state of things — something radically wrong which wants a change.

"Consistency, thou art a jewel,"

whose sparkling and glittering are not tarnished by much wear in this field of usefulness, as yet.

We want a higher standard of knowledge, and all the avenues opened wide and clear which lead to it, and all the others closed. These laws, if once made, will without doubt be maintained by the people whom they are most intended to benefit. The people are ready to petition the Legislature upon these vital subjects and set us and themselves right, and destroy these glaring inconsistencies.

These laws, then, if passed, will tend to make us better. We can still improve by other ways than outside pressure or legal enactments. Our system of medical associations and medical societies have done much to improve our standing and knowledge: those organizations have but recently been invented, and it has not always been the case that the labor done in those societies was well economized. But as they are year by year maturing, extending and in every way impoving, they come to be a great success.

ASSOCIATION.

When a person wants to express the superlative strength there is in association, he may do so most successfully by first putting upon exhibition the comparatively puerile results of individual effort. However much we may admire the grandeur and magnificence of independent individuality, yet an association of such in concert of supporting action, is as incomparably superior to all the ends of force—physical, moral or mental—as the great receptacle of waters — the ocean — is to the brooklet.

Inasmuch as God has placed upon the brow of each individual of the broad earth, a countenance, singular to each, to which no other can claim exact resemblance, so in the evolutious and endowments of their physical and mental organizations, the same disparity is observed to exist; and from such differences issue the great and conflicting diversity of thought and action which, when associated in one grand, harmonious whole, constitute the ifinity of brains of the universe and

the insurmountable and irresistable momentum
of the physical world. We are vastly deficient
in those disinterested faculties which cultivate
and court the influences emanating from association. Our individual selfishness induce us to
conceal our lights beneath the staves, and thus
circumscribed, by narrow limits, stultify and
smother, and in many instances those circumstan-
tial gifts of opportunity and accident, which, in
the hands of competent help would have been
beacon blazes of intelligence and blessings to the
world of human beings yet destined to grope in
the continual darkness of ten thonsand ages,
simply for the want of such assistance.

We view the single drop of water and wonder
at its many singularities and inherent qualities;
we see it falling from on high and in its passage
paint, in prismatic dyes upon the darkened back-
ground of the thundering heavens, the bow of
promise; diving into its integral elements by
microscopic lenses, we see its countless quantities
of globes, each capable of being inhabited by
millions of animalcules, and spreading these out
to still fairer view by chemical analysis, we find
that oxygen, hydrogen and steam are to be in-
vestigated before we can comprehend the sum-total
of its magnificent minutæ. Now, assemble this
miniature world with its kind in quantities to
constitute the "babbling brook" which schoolboys
dam with but a wisp and stop its flow until it
gathers, by association, a power outstretching
childish ingenuity and strength, and bursts its
bands to seek its object of election by aggregation
with others on their course, until the family in-
flation amounts to rivers, broad, deep interminable

contributors to

"The Image of Eternity—
The Throne of the Invisible.".

And the difference there is between isolated
drops and oceans, is as the difference between one
man's efforts, unassisted by the labors and past
experiences of others, and the congregated stores
of knowledge and all the associated influences
arranged and displayed in systematic order.
Consider this difference and this comparison for
one moment. And by way of illustration! Take
the infant, born with the brains of a Webster, if
you will, and the ambition of a Napoleon, and
isolate him from human influences and association,
simply teaching him to talk and take his healthy
exercises and supports of life in vigor; and thus
should he be turned loose, like Robinson Cruso,
upon a world, even in lieu of an island, our hopes
of the results of his life's labors would be meager
and puerile, and the substantiation of those hopes
even but a mythical dream. Give him, on the
other hand, the world for intercommunion; let
him stand, for a starting point, upon the culmi-
nating intelligences of the earth as it now is,
guide him by all available genius, and thus mailed,
present to him the sealed lids which cover the
untraversed realms of undiscovered sciences, supported by the intellectual strength of those eru-
dite fathers in letters, who labor to accomplish
also in his line, and we have for this, as a report, a glowing description of accomplishments
transcending expectations, a colossal engorge-
ment of mental and physical results, captiva-
ting and magnificent beyond the grasp of hope,

of which, when the report is made, so much falls short of the true influences and effects to succeeding ages, that he who in the cycling centuries, seeks the history of this man's movements and of those who supported him, pronounces upon their merits, after the test of time, in the language of Solomon at the completion of his temple, and while standing in its eastern porch, viewing its magnificence and grandeur, and filled with admiration and praise, turned to his master workman with his highest compliment, and exclaimed:

"Rabboni!—Most Excellent Master!"

Thus it is seen in salient distinction the vast difference between associated and single effort. The one all insignificant and impotent; the other incomprehensibly powerful and grand beyond conception.

And we who are associated thus, for medical improvement, are driving on in those swelling channels which ever lead "onward and upward."

And now, ladies and gentlemen, there is but one more subject which I wish to lug into this poly-headed text; and this one I cannot say will make us better and am far from srying will make us worse, yet it is one we will surely have to meet in our daily rounds of busy life.

The eastern firmament is presenting to view a constellation of new stars, gossimer-gilded and all-glorious, who westward, with that which was the consort of Empire, took its way, will reach us ere long, and the citizens of all our western towns will soon see fair woman pracicing medicine.

And why not?

THE WOMEN AS DOCTORS.

When one comes to canvas the privileges to be awarded to the ladies, it is always best to be found patronizing the side of the most extensive plans of prudential decorum, and these are to let them manage their own affairs as they may in their ripe judgement desire; always giving whatever rank and occupation in society they ask; arranging laws and customs granting them the most perfect equality in all things, and leaving them to govern their own proprietory conduct, feeling assured that, although long trails may, "in life's young dream," outrage common sense "for a wee short hour," yet the more stately pride in the female heart, after this "fitful fever" of flimsey fashion, will rise in dominant command and "the feast of reason and flow of soul" will reign, serene and majestic; by virtue of the persuasive power of female prestige, as the production of the most fastidious element in any society beneath the angels, the labor of imperious regulators — queens-par-excellent — of the social circle.

We will make the promise for Decatur, that if ever the day dawns upon her prosperous and progressive people when a doctor emanating from among band-boxes and crinoline, and burnished in the velvet of the softer sex shall seek to locate here, qualified and capable for the accomplishment of professional demands, that not one member of this proverbially jealous profession now here and of this society, will be found to interpose one objection to the new intrusion, but will gracefully abide by the voice of democracy and improve with them as the lessons of reform roll on. We promise them a free field and a fair engagement; and if at the close the victory be theirs, it will the more pointedly prove the movement to be established in right.

It comes with poor grace from us who have always, perhaps unconsciously, been absorbing lessons in propriety from those most competent to give, and who have ever been consistent with their own teachings, while yet those lessons are as much needed as ever before, to convert ourselves into a "grand army of occupation" to prevent the ladies from committing acts of indelicacy, One might think we were ungallant enough in thus acting to do so from interested motives. We therefore want it expressly understood that, in our humble judgement, the day is here when women will do their part in all great literary and professional pursuits as they desire, and that we are very much in favor of their having that privilege. One thing is certain, as a half dozen recent wars have proved in as many different nations, that if any philanthropic lighthouse on the fair face of the earth can dart rays and beams and floods of living light and hope and permanent pleasure into the disconsolate souls of the sick and suffering, it is that which radiates from the presence and conduct of an honest, self-sacrificing and concientious woman, while in the accomplishment of her charitable considerations for the afflicted in hospitals and districts destitute of the very things her munificence provides, Those who suffered thus, as thousands have in many instances, remember longer and better the circumstances of her angel visit and kind offers, than the hours of anguish which called

APPENDIX.

her spontaneous compassions to their assistance.

These offices are the natural growth of the female heart and are God's own ground-work reflecting the soul of the true woman: and Chicago has them; and Cairo has them; and Danville and Quincy have them; and all the towns, cities, villages, hamlets and counties within this circle have them; they are every where, and in every place available to these very ends. Go anywhere within the border of Illinois, or any patriot State which joins her, and ask a wounded or sick soldier if he remembers Decatur, having once in such condition passed the place, and their first inquiry will be concerning the wellfare of that little band of basket-bearers who always bore them articles of comfort and words of hope and cheer, and made them proud of their wounds though death stood threatening through them. I could call their names: I see them here: they honor us this dreary night with their majestic presence—long may they live to know and feel our high regard for them.

I hope and pray for the perfection of the medical profession; and with the approximation of that end in view, would gladly introduce to her various departments as many discordant elements; as much harmony and strength; as many stand-points of observation; as much versatility of talents; as much honorable competition and rivalry; as much conflict of judgment; as broad a determination to pioneer in unscaled fields where the genius of science and the energy of man has never before traversed since they fell from the plastic hand of God; as much disinterested and careful criticism; as many creeds and colors, shades and kinds as are to be comprehended in all the grades of life, from savage to civelised, for in the language of the immortal Jefferson "truth has nothing to fear from error if left free to combat it." And with all this contrariety of talent; these guards; all these elements stimulating to investigation; we would look for the column of the monument of medicine to rise' strong, straight and stately—a colossal edifice, embellished with the inscriptions of the most absolute facts; crowned with a capital borne so high in the atmosphere of universal letters that it shall be the pride, the glory and the hope of all the languages of the earth.

And would letting fair woman into the ranks of medicine, subtract one jot from the sublimity and perfection of this picture? Has she ever blasted by ignominy, incompetence, ignorance or infidelity any enterprise to which she has turned her fair hand and heart? Has any thing or nation or science or sect or religion ever prospered on the earth and under God, against which her honest Christ-like weight of character was cast? No, gentlemen! and we warn you now, that when she yearns to become a doctor, and God knows we wish her no such calamiy, yet if she shall ever desire to cruise in our professional gulf with her missionary craft—we should say, like the hero of short courtships, in David Copperfield, "Barkis is willing."

APPENDIX.

Inauguration of the V. C. & M. R. W.

For more than a year past the English Company, having the construction of this important work in hand, have been pushing it forward after the fashon of true American zeal under the supervision of Mr. Crawly, with Mr. Thomas Braniff as generalisimo of the field forces. During this year they have constructed near 100 miles of the road over the Sierra Madre mountains; and when the work is comprehended by a thorough inspection, it is truly astonishing to see that, small mortals as we are, such seeming impossibilities have been so briefly dispatched. Mountains, rivers, gorges, plains and valleys have been traversed by the track for the trains; and on the first day of January, 1873, a party of 1,000 persons left the city of Mexico to inspect and pronounce upon the great acomplishment. President Lerdo with 700 invited guests, and many others, constituted this inspection party, and sailed out in two triumphant trains, full of glee, enthusiasm, patriotism and some cognac of course, and safely reached this city on the sea, on the evninge of the second. Great preparations had been made to receive the visitors, and to provide such entertainments as would make them remember Vera Cruz with sensations of joy and gratitude; and in all these the liberal, courteous and urbane citizens of this Port have certainly accomplished a great success.

Prisident Lerdo, although born at Jalapa, had never seen the gulf. His visit on this occasion was extremely opportune, as the weather presented all its peculiarities in the four days of his stay in the city. He had receptions, dances, dinners, bonfire, illuminations, beautiful fire-works, a sea voyage, a shipwreck; a Norther, and he enjoyed them all with that placid zest which so plainly marks the truly great mind. Flags floated from houses, offices, forts and all the shipping, and when the President moved, cannons were fired, brilliantly uniformed military awaited to escort him, and every attention systematically placed at his disposition.

The hotels were insufficient for the entertainment of the crowd and private citizens threw open thier houses to their friends, and at these places, the enthusiasm assailed the domestic circles, and like a tidal wave of pleasure, glorified the poplace. The reporters of the Press have given the pudlic programs, speaches, and entertainments, but these private corners, where in the "feast of reason and flow of soul" found ready vent

APPENDIX.

could not be ntoiced. One, however, met
our ear at a dinner party at the U. S. Consulate — the sentiment and speach being
given by the Consul as follows

A TOAST:
EVEN THE SPIRIT OF BAALAM S ASS REJOICES WITH US.

"This is an age of oddities let loose" on Mexico.
A new Star in the East has arisen which betokens
the birth of a Messenger whose beneficent employment will be to develope a new departure for
the rich resources of this great country. This new
born Missionary is the completion of the Vera
Cruz and Mexico Railway; and its mission will
be to encourage civilization in all its branches of
Agriculture, Commerce, Manufacture, the domestic concord, harmony and intelligence of the citizen;
and all the achievements which go to establish
the worth, wealth and prosperity of a nation.

In the completion of this vast enterprise, all
those who have underwent the bruise inflicted
upon both body and soul by a trip in a stage
coach from this city to the Capitol, should thank
God in deep humility and great earnestness for
as much of said body and soul as is left uncon-
sumed after the passage of the perilous ordeal.
And they are entitled to be joined by the people
of this salubrious land in loud hosannas for the
dawning glories of this auspicious day. Yea,
verily: it is for even more than man to rejoice!
Even the Spirit of Baalam's Ass rejoices with us.
The day of Jubilee for the mule and the donkey
has arrived; and did their dormant natures know
of the pageantry of this day, they would greet
you in their dulcet brayings, not as their ancestor

talked to Baalam, but in glad rejocings for their emancipation from the cruel loads which have for so many murderous years oppressed them. And in behalf of the mule, and for Mr. Berg, I volunteer a recognition of an act tending towards a suppression of cruelty to animals; and for them I offer congratulations and acknowledgements for the fate which promises them a change for the better.

This grand procession, this triumphant train from the National Capitol this day, is the funeral cortege of the Stage Coach, the forty-mule team and the Pack Train, for the section over which the procession has passed. Those are things, henceforth, to be numbered among the obsolete, and as having been superceeded by appliances of civilization equal to the intelligence, energy and enterprise of the Nineteenth Century.

Mexico should feel proud of this great work; and that she does so, the presence of the Chief Magistrate and these Honorable Guests are sufficient proof.

Veracruzanos! Imagine your astonishment and that of your children, ten years hence, on hearing a description of a huge leviathan of a mud-road wagon attempting to do the herculean labor of a railroad! I would advise you to detail your good historians to draw a graphic portraiture of the times when such things existed; and often to compare it with the new condition as time and improvements roll on. It will strengthen your zeal for progressive civilization, and give you renewed opportunities to thank God that the English Company and Thomas Braniff have had an existance in Mexico.

Mexico, June 18. 1874

Hon. S. T. Trowbridge,

U. S. Consul, Veracruz.

Dear Sir;

You are hereby invited to join in a dinner to be given, in this city on the 4th day of July next, and to extend the invitation to all other Americans in Vera Cruz who may desire to assist in commemorating the day. A number of distinguished persons will be invited, including the President, Cabinet and Foreign Ministers.

The amount of individual subscription will be about $8.

Please reply as soon as convenient as to yourself and others,

Yours Truly,

J. W. Foster.
G. S. Skilton.
N. A. Rector.
C. C. Gaugh.

} **COMMITTEE.**

U. S. Consulate, Vera Cruz,
June 24. 1874.

Hon. John W. Foster, Geo. S. Skilton,
N. A. Rector and Mr. Gaugh;

Gentlemen:

Yours of June 18., inviting the
American citizens of Vera Cruz to a banquet in
honor of the 98. Anniversary of American Independence to be given in in the City of Mexico,
has been received and circulated, and some three
or four are promising themselves the great pleasure of an attendance. I am sorry that I cannot be
one of the number, yet so the wheel of fortune
revolves for me. Five long years have been
counted off since I have seen a FOURTH of JULY
on Native Amrican soil, and it is as when our
friends depart from us and go hence into the
world or out of it, that our memories cherish
the better elements of their natures until naught
but the good remains to revive and support the
love we bear for "Auld Lang Syne." So when
one leaves the prosperous land of the happy
Yankee and wanders even in a Sister Republic

"Where the Rose and the Mango grow gratis for love,"

he finds that for those passing years, with his
first affections left in the colder climate, that as
the time rolls on, the planted seed of "Hail
Columbia" grows on new soil — engrafted as one

may say — to increase with a more savory flavor and of grander proportions, forgetting the exceptionable qualities, and remembering, with fonder affection, only Brother Johnathan and Uncle Samuel "AT HOME," whose birth days both happened to come off on that same auspicious morning just 98 years ago, at that celebrated Tea Party in Boston. You know we were all born at tea parties; some at Posey county Indiana, some in "Egypt" Illinois, while others had their baggage packed in Troy. Dr. Warren was the attending physician at that Boston party, and his babes and their Alma Mater did as well as could be expected; but the operation killed the Doctor. And to honor and perpetuate the growing glory of Dr. Warren, I send you a sentiment touching his reputable offspring.

"A full bumper to those two prosperous and healthy youngsters, Brother Johnathan and Uncle Samuel: may their families increase in their land, and may they sow no more Wild Oats."

Knowing that you are happy and sober, I send you my greetings, Gentlemen, and God be with you on THE FOURTH.

Yours Truly,

S. T. TROWBRIDGE.

Printed by Hattie.

APPENDIX.

With the characteristic urbanity constituting the esprit of Mr. Thomas Braniff,
Superintendent of the Vera Cruz and Mexico Rail Way Company, we the undersigned and family were complimented with a
pass to Mexico and return—dead-headed,
in railroad phraseology—and on the 2d of
May 1874, we railed out, seven jolly Desde-
monias and one sober Benedict, to see the
truly great sights on a trip from Vera
Cruz to Mexico. The writer has, on a
previous occasion, given his observations as
made on a journey by diligence to the same
historic city, but now as the railroad is completed and in splendid condition, passing
other fields of immense interest it is but fair
to suppose that if it were possible to give a
clear and comprehensive description of the
observable features of this most delightful
thoroughfare, it might be interesting to all
those friends of the writer who have the inclination and patience to read it. I hope it
may do even more. For while those possessing the time, means and disposition to
amuse themselves by a trip of recreation, do
so almost every year by going to Lake

Superior, Saratoga, the White Mountains, California, Europe, or some of the many seasides or sulphur springs, they but little know that so closely at hand and so securely accessible are sights, climates, entertainments in this magnificent country, lying open to the blazing sun, ready for any sight-seeing swain to take convulsions over, if beauty, grandeur and magnificence ever produce that effect. For those far-seeing and matter-of-fact mamas who have marriageable daughters to dispose of at good bargains, I am not recommending this road of travel, but to those who want to see beautiful and strange sights—passingly strange and gorgeously beautiful—this is the richest route in everything that will longest abide by the recollections and with brightest satisfactions of any one a tourist may advance upon for a two months voyage in any season of the year. If you wish to escape the snows of zero, come to Mexico. If you wish to shun the torrid heat of summer, come to Mexico, for here you have a climate to your choice, even to the fraction of a degree. If you want variety, then half a day by rail or a day in diligence, or on horseback, and the whole range of climatic changes are wrought from everlasting snow to unceasing tropical heat. Travelers

who have seen all tell me that the richness
of scenery of Switzerland, the Alps and
the Rocky Mountains are all concentrat-
ed in the Sierra Madre over which the
railroad runs. While I can testify that our
Alleghanies are incomparably insignificant·
Here, with all the loveliness of natural scenery is a constant change of characters and
customs, so peculiar and engrossing to one
who has never witnessed it, that he is always thinking himself in some far-off Af-
ghanistan or Central Africa. wondering
one short week could possibly have transported him so far from his old associations.
You start from Vera Cruz at 2, A. M.—
a very seasonable hour for those who wish
to escape the nightmares of the small hours,
but usually very pleasant if the want of sleep
be not very pressing in as much as it is always fresh and cool at that hour and the
sea breeze most invigorating. Then, if it
be moonlight in the full—but I can no
more describe it than Parrhasius could paint
a dying groan—so glorious are the moonlit
heavens in these tropical regions. We of
the temperate zone only receive slanting
rays of that "pale Cynthia" which in the e-
quatorial districts becomes a full effulgent
beamer capable of dispelling the somber
shades to such a degree that the finest print

may easily be read by no other than her soft
though sinful rays of light.   Over plains
studded with a scrubby,thinly set and dwarf-
ed growth of tree, suggesting the idea of an
irregularly planted peach orchard, filled
with volcanic rocks, black, porous and bowl-
der shaped; you glide for the first 50 miles,
when you strike the foot of the first range
of mountains, called the Chiquihuitas. Up
to this very point the railroad has been
straight and very level—though in reality
you have ascended a thousand feet—more
or less slightly it may be.   But here the
grade is augmented to 4 per centum for a
stretch of nearly a league, when you have
gained a giddy height, and as if defiant at a
further invitation to ascend, the engine dash-
es full drive, directly into and through the
corner of a precipitous crag at the crest of
the mountain through the first of the 16 long
dark tunnels along the road.   On emerg-
ing from this tunnel, as if shot from a breech
loading columbiad, you are bulged into an
amphitheater of cascades, precipices, mountains, railroad bridges and tunnels; wild, da-
zing and beautiful, far, far beyond the power of any explanatory pen-painting.   Your
speed at this point is perhaps less than 8
miles per hour and gives a brief sojourn in
this beautiful vista. In all these wild moun-

ain views you can hardly change your position a single rod without obliterating the old
pictures for the entirely new field of sights,
giving transient glimpses of them as you pass
along, like the revolutions of a kaleidoscope
with its ever changing new formations of
prismatic crystals. I can hardly bear to pass
this field of beauty without attempting to item
ize its various points of attraction. You are
over 250 feet perpendicular above the foam
ing cascade, on a bridge, one tunnel behind
you, and the engine just entering another;
the mountain many hundred feet above you,
rugged, rock bound and threatening, and
just across the chasm another mountain,
probably 2000 ft. high and apparently within
stone throw of the car window at which you
sit, spell bound and transfixed with awe and
admiration. Then, suddenly, all is dark as
night, and you have passed the second tunnel and the highest point of the Chiquihui-
ta. We rush now over rich agricultural districts—wanting the agriculture however,—
pass Cordova and vast fields of timber with
a heavy undergrowth of coffee and all class-
es of grain and tropical fruits and next come
to the Metlac Baranca. This is a deep gulch
traversed by a small stream; the engineers
first attempted crossing it at right angles.
This would have necessitated the construc-

tion of a monster iron suspension bridge 1.
500 feet long and 500 feet high; but rather
than carry out this first design, they changed the plat, and turning up the right side of
the bluffs cut a serpentine way for the track
in the mountain side, and descended at a
four and one half per cent grade for two
miles, until they found a narrow point for
crossing, and built a semicircular bridge of
much strength and beauty, and thus gaining
the opposite bank, turned again down the
stream, though up another four and a half
per cent grade at the side of the bluffs, until they reached the point opposite to the
commencement of the deflection: then,
straight on to the westward to Orizava City. This Metlac Baranca is very exciting-
ly beautiful. One feels much of the time
while passing it as if sailing in mid air, nor
knowing where or how to alight, if at all.
Orizava is a city of about 12000 inhabitants
intensely catholic. She is surronnded by
mountains bearing salient marks of volcanic
actions and yielding to the geologist a grand
field of rich reward for his researches. I
should have said that at the foot of the Chiquihuitas we changed our Rodgers engine
for an English double ender, i.e. two engines in one, of immense size and weight
invented by Mr. Fairley. This is is the i-

ron horse destined to take us to the top of the mountains yet many hundred feet above us, to Boca del Monte. There has been a great strife between the representatives of the locomotive interests of England and the United States; for the past year. The mechanics of each nation here claiming the post of excellence. It is still an open question although some trials have at least been very flattering to U. S. machines, as a third rate Baldwin engine took up the mountain, as many cars and as heavy loads as a first rate Fairley has ever taken, and did it with much less fuel and two thirds the pressure of steam in the same or less time. Orizava is the great machine shop depot of the road where may be seen English, American, German, French and Mexican mechanics laboring in great harmony and with much skill. From Orizava to Boca del Monte are about 9 leagues or 26 miles, and every foot of the road is replete with picturesque views, worth the journey of a Continent. If I have had the temerity to attempt a description of the Chiquihuitas and Metlac Baranca. and feel as I do, that the effort is a blank failure, I can certainly not expect to succeed in conveyin even the faintest outline of a correct idea of this part of the journey. In fact. I only do so hoping that

what is said will induce those voyagers in
quest of pleasure to come and see for them
selves the true pictures to be so cheaply
seen. Then, they can know that no pen
painting genius can ever rise to the capabil
ity of the task. The mountains are higher,
more rocky and rugged; the railroad runs
over more dangerous curves and precipices;
the sceneries and landscapes around grow
more extensive and varied; the stratas of
rocks form new and different geological out-
croppings; the botanical growths present
new species; you are much nearer to Orizava, the monarch of all the lesser mountains,
and in fine your head will ache and your
eyes tire, as ours did, with the active effort
to see it all and attempt to fix the dissolv-
ing perspectives on the canvas of memory.
You have left the Tierra Caliente or Hot
Country, and are inhaling a cool, ice- chill-
ed breeze from the snows of centuries on
the crest of Orizava. This grand old white
headed patriarch is the ever embellishing
figure head of all the views, or most of them
which are presented between the city of
Orizava and far on the plains beyond the top
of the Sierra Madres. Between Orizava
city and Maltrata, the next station, is the
gulch called "El Inficrno" which signifies
"Hell" and is doubtless a more formidable

place than that from which the Biblical Hades at the rear of Old Jerusalem took its name, and from which this canon derives its title. If the cars were to jump the track at this place, they would certainly descend nearly a quarter of a mile and bring up in a better or a worse world, and the name this place bears is not inviting. Maltrata is a small place composed chiefly of R. R. buildings, and is just at the foot of the principal range of mountains, in a narrow valley of from 50 rods to three quarters of a mile in width. This valley is agriculturally occupied by small farmers, cultivating small fields which, beheld from the 2500 feet elevation soon gained after leaving Maltrata, look like so many gardens not larger than a 25 by 50 feet grass plot. Maltrata is about 6000 feet above the sea. From Maltrata to Boen del Monte is only 2 miles direct, but the railroad on reaching the latter place rises 2500 feet and traverses 17 miles of the sides of the mountain to reach it. All this distance of 17 miles presents a constant succession of magnificent views far exceeding any thing yet encountered on this interesting thoroughfare. To construct the railroad there as substantially as it has been done, was a most masterly piece of engineering. The cars glide smoothly and very noiseless-

ly up the serpentine curves, and the speed
being so slow one feels very secure, even
though the head turns giddy at the perpendicular distances bewildering the sight.

These heights, curves, hills and valleys,
these rocks, rivulets, ridges and this railroad
are all contributors to the plenitude of the
amphitheater. Our little three and a half
year old Maudie, on looking out of the car
window at the exalting panorama, said,
when all was hushed by the imposing grandeur surrounding us: "¡O, que buen pais!"–
Oh! what a beautiful country!–She was en-
cored by every passenger in the car saying:
" bien dicho." And surely the little traveler
had a good subject on which to exercise the
smooth Castilian language. We ascended
through clouds and rainbows lending their
haloes to the enchanting scenes When
you arrive at Boca del Monte you can look
down at Maltrata, two miles distant, and
houses and horses seem like children's toys
of the same articles spread out upon a car-
pet. When we returned from Mexico and
descended this winding inclined plane, I
was invited by the engineer to ride down on
the locomotive. The invitation was gladly
accepted, and gave me splendid facilities for
observing all these fields of interests with
unobstructed sight. I could not help picturing

to myself the horror of accident, if that dire
day must come, to any train leaving the
track and dashing itself to atoms from so
many dangerous points along the way. But
every precaution is exercised to prevent disastrous casualities. The road is constantly
and thoroughly inspected and is, as already
stated, most substantially constructed; the
engines and cars are critically examined before leaving Orizaba; none but the most expert and trustworthy men take charge, or
are employed on this part of the road; and
the rate of speed is limited to from 4 to
6 miles per hour. Therefore, the chances
for accident are reduced to the smallest possibility. Here are no intense frosts to in-
tervene with complicating circumstances.
At Boca del Monte we part with our strong
friend, the Fairley Double-ender, and are
pulled now by a Belgian or French engine
to Mexico. The country after leaving the
top of the mountain at Boca del Monte is
quite level and much of it is devoted to agriculture. Though mountains are on both
sides, and now Orizava is behind you, there
soon present to view three other perpetual
snow bearing mountains, Malincha, Yzstacyhuatl and Popocatapelt. Near San Mar-
cus all these venerable whiteheads may be
seen at once. That soul is dull, indeed

which is not moved with enthusiastic delight at these tombstones of volcanic convulsions which the earth endured in centuries long past. Popocatapetl is 19000 ft. high. Yzstacyhuatl or "The White Woman in her Shrouds" is 17000, Orizava also 17000 feet high ard Malincha just reaching the snow zone—is occasionally seen without snow. Orizava is in a chain of mountais while the others appear to have raised from the plain. Popocatapetl and the White Woman are only 20 miles apart, and the former though in the shape of a sugar loaf and apparently the steepest. of all is the easiest of ascent· except Malincha. It will be remembered that Cortez with his army passed between Popocatapetl and the White Woman and ordered 20 of his men to ascend Popocatapetl in order to show the natives the power and perseverence of the invaders. After Cortez had conquered Montezuma, and captured his mistress, he carried her to the Malincha mountain where he sold her to one of his generals. This woman's name was Malincha, and ever after this kidnapping occurrence the mountain has borne that appellation. Mr. Foster, our Honorable Minister at Mexico, now owns the writing-desk on which the contract between Cortez and his general, concerning the marriage was written. It is a beautiful piece of furniture, composed of different kinds of wood, peculiar to Mexico; and most artistically constructed.—The richness of the soil of the valleys of Mexico and Puebla, so much talked and written about by historians, appears to the Illinois man like a desert waste, and I must confess I was greatly disappointed in my expectations of its appearance and produce. It bears the Megue or American Aloe, a Cactus from which large quantities of Pulque are manufactured and, also tolerably, a kind of sedge grass as well as wheat, barley, rye, oats and corn, yet very poorly indeed. The farmers use the same kind of implements employed by our Mosaic ancestors, and can no more be moved to improvements in these implements than you can move the mountains. Their ancestral delineation and religion forbid any change. Their horses, cattle, sheep, hogs and dogs are of a scrubby mustang species. Cats and fighting fowls, however, flourish finely as the nocturnal concerts of either will prove on any night of the year. They tie up their hogs, and turn loose their donkeys. By the most extraordinary slight of hand work they succeed in milking the most aqueous preparations from their cows and goats to be found in any civilized country.

We reach the city of Mexico at 9 o'clock P. M. The hotels of the city are very good and their charges for service and fare are reasonable. We staid there only 4 days, and one of them was a Sunday, another a holiday—the 5. of May.—We visited the Alameda, Tacobaya, Chipultepec, The Paseo, The Noche Triste, The Academy of Arts, The Palace, The American Cemetery, Guadelupe, The Cathedral, The U. S. Legation and Consulate; saw, where Alverado made his big jump when chased by the Aztecs; saw the President, the Aqueducts, the battle fields of Cherobusco, Contreas, Molino del rey, Chipultepec, Ciudadela and Mexico, all glorions with the remembrance of American bravery in 1847; saw the "cinco del Mayo" celebration, the military and civil force of the Capitol, the fireworks at night; in fine, the city and citizens in this her gayest season. Now, shall I tell you something of each of these things and places? If you want to hear it, read on; if not, consider my narration ended at this point, for our dead-head compliment from Mr. Braniff took us safely back to Vera Cruz, sin novedad.

THE ALAMEDA

Is a park, large and beautiful, with native forest trees, fountains, walks, flowers, statues &c. &c. The citizens display great taste and affection for children, for here are seen miniature railroad trains filled with little boys and girls and pulled by men, velocipedes, bicycles and tricycles, small omnibusses with the same motive power as the small cars and carriages pulled by goats and sheep. Music is daily played in this park, at all events was while we were there, it being holiday times.

TACUBAYA.

We visited this suburban city situated about 4 miles S. W. of Mexico with the Hon. J. W. Foster, U. S. Minister, to Mexico and lady. Mr. Foster had a pass to see the residences of Mr. Escandon and Mr. Barron. We went only through the grounds of the first named gentleman. This is a beautiful country residence filled with fine statuary and paintings. The grounds are very picturesque and artistic, with lakes, rivulets, grottoes, fine forest trees, native and exotic plants, shrubs and flowers and swans on the lakes.

CHIPULTEPEC.

The same party visited Chipultepec. This is truly a place of much historic interest. It is a high hill 3 miles westward of

Mexico, with a palace upon its summit built by the viceroys of Spain when they ruled the country. This palace was their residence and is now government property and the "White House" of Mexico, or the President's residence. This palace is now undergoing repairs and, therefore, unoccupied. We ascended 229 steps to reach its highest part or battlement, and stood where Baron von Humboldt was standing when he said: "The sight from the top of the town of Chipultepec is the finest vista on the earth." From this beautiful eminence you can look down upon the city of Mexico, can see the valley of Mexico, Cherobusco, Contreras, Molino del rey, Guadelupe, Los Remedios, Tacubaya, Popocatapetl and Yzstacyhuatl. 60 miles distant and on a clear bay so plain that you would feel assured they were but 5 miles off, and nearer: the ranges of small mountains each with volcanic craters thickly studded are silently telling the scientist of the fires which were once burning in the bosom of the earth but now are extinct forever. Here, under the view of him who stands on the Palace of Chipultepec is the place where the pilgrimaging Aztecs found the fulfillment of their prophecy; that they would found a city on the place where they would encounter an eagle sitting on a cactus and eating a snake and there they would close their wanderings. They say that here, indeed, they saw that apparition in the middle of a shallow lake. Who ever saw a cactus grow in a lake? At all events, and probably for the sake of safety, they built the present capital in the centre. From here may be seen those beautiful lakes gleaming at a distance like sheets of pure silver while they intensely disgust you as you sail on their turbid surface and have an opportunity for close inspection. Your historic recollections are reviving of times when human sacrifices were made to appease the wrath of stone idols which superstition invested with relentless power; when the Inquisition suppressed the sacrifices, but did not lessen the flow of blood; when wars after wars and treacheries and scenes of horror passed over the stage which now, lies before you, an idyl of serenity and peace. I could not help thinking how much blood brutally has been spilt and how many barbarities have been committed in this beautiful valley and asked: Who among all the actors in that drama has left a name to guide the denizens of this human hive to better actions by his example?—But we could not stop here long enough to think it all over for Prescott

and dame Calderon &c &c rushed through
our memories and we retreated to examine
the beautiful though indecent statuary of
the unfortunate Austrian prince who played
here his brief part as emperor; we also,
looked at the grounds below us. At the
base of Chipultepec is a big tree, 42 ft.
in circumference at 5 ft. above the ground.
It is a monstrous cypress, named "Montezuma." There is a cave or subterranean
passage from the base of Chipultepec leading deep into the hill and up to the palace.
It looks like a dark passage leading to dark
designs.

THE PASEO.

It is a fine carriage drive between the
city and Chipultepec and every fine evening
may be seen hundreds of carriages fraught
with the aristocratic beauties of the city.
Soldiers, guards and police are in full attendance and if you listen to the reports
of thefts and robberies you will hardly wonder at the precaution.

I pass over a description of all the points
enumerated except Guadelupe, as the
mere mention of the names, as has been
given is deemed sufficient.

The followers of Cortez could not hold
the religious power he wanted to exercise

over the minds of the natives by the introduction of the foreign element of faith as
taught by images of the virgin Mary in
their temples. Therefore, they invented
the novel idea of having the virgin reappear
on earth and they say she did so at the site
where now stands the chapel bearing her
new name of Guadalupe. It is about 3 and
one half miles N. E. of the city, situated
on a hill just on the spot, they claim as the
one where the virgin thrice showed herself
to a poor Indian shepherd. This transaction naturalized the virgin and rendered her
the popular deity of all the Mexicans. At
the base of the hill where the chapel is built
is a very large spring of Chalybeate and
Magnesian water, highly medicinal and
which bears the reputation of being the
place where Guadalupe put her foot on
the only occasion she put it down in this
country. The halt, the lame, the blind,
the lazy, the leprous mortals come crawling
to this shrine to be healed of the maladies of
body and soul by this holy water. Miracles
are almost daily attributed to the answer to
prayer offered up to Guadalupe, and those
miracles are placarded in the large cathedral as an advertisement in proof of the in-
fallibility of her Saintship's powers. All
this stuff and disgusting trumpery has the

sanction of the Infallible Pope of Rome.
As proof to this read his maledictions a-
gainst the governments of Mexico and Gua-
temala who wanted to throw off such un-
cleanliness.

I did not enjoy the climate of the city.
The situation is too high; the air too light
and dry. The temperature is 62 for all the
year round and not 5 degrees variation.
Your lungs feel oppressed and two of our
party had attacks of bleeding at the nose
(**Epistaxis**) whenever they ascended high
flights of steps. It is a fatal mistake for
weak lunged patients to go to the city of
Mexico for relief.

At "low twelve" the train leaves for Vera Cruz: and after four days enjoyment at
a place where as many weeks might be
spent with pleasure and profit we parted
from kind and extremely attentive friends,
descended from above the clouds, and landed
at 5.40 P. M. within the walls of Vera
Cruz, with our lives elongated and our
souls improved, as we hope, by our six days
ramble among the Aztecs.

S. T. T.

Pres. by

Lorin O. Thompson

Shawnee Classics
A Series of Classic Regional Reprints for the Midwest